You Must Know the Times

Answers to 25 Essential Questions on

End Time Prophecy

Dennis James Woods

LIFE TO LEGACY

You Must Know the Times
Answers to 25 Essential Questions On End Time Prophecy

by Dennis James Woods, Copyright ©2020
Revised 2021

ISBN-13: 978-947288-59-1

Printed in the United States
10 9 8 7 6 5 4 3 2 1

Cover design by: Legacy Design Inc
        Legacydesigninc@gmail.com

Published by
Life To Legacy, LLC
P.O. 1239
Matteson, IL 60443
877-267-7477
www.Life2Legacy.com
Life2legacybooks@att.net

CONTENTS

ACKNOWLEDGMENTS

I would like to give special thanks to my lovely wife Chantia. Her moral support, prayers, and companionship has enriched every aspect of my life. To all of our Podcast, Zoom, and radio listeners, you keep me motivated to be the best I can be. To those who attended bible study at my home, your thirst for truth both encouraged and challenged me. To all of my ministerial friends and associates, your brotherly love is strengthening because iron sharpens iron. And finally, thanks to Elder Ronald Smith whose sermons encouraged everyone by exhorting, "you must know the times."

This book is dedicated to all those who thirst and hunger for "what thus saith the Lord."

Introduction

Let me be clear on what the purpose is for this book. This book is not designed to answer every question about the vast subject of eschatology, the study of end time prophecy. This book was not written to explain every eschatological doctrine. This book is not intended to be a verse-by-verse commentary on the Book of Revelation. This book is not written to sensationalize the end times, nor trying to find prophetic fulfillment in every news headline.

It is the author's intention that this book be an aid to individuals who are seeking to gain a working knowledge of what the Bible teaches about the end times. As most of us know, there are many opposing views and erroneous doctrines all surrounding the last days. In years past, there have been many who have attempted to predict the day of the rapture, and have been wrong one-hundred percent of the time. Then again, there are those who will exploit any event and see prophetic fulfillment behind every catastrophe.

For example, in the year 2020, the world was confronted with the COVID-19 pandemic. In 2021, then the *delta variant* struck. No one could have predicted the devastating impact this novel virus would have on the world. Millions of people were infected worldwide. In America alone, over 600,000 people died. In addition to the death toll, national economies were on the brink of collapsing. People were forbidden to leave their homes and required to practice social distancing, and wear masks. Schools, churches, malls, sports events, and most public gatherings were prohibited or greatly reduced. All these mandated precautions gave cause to conspiracy theorists and end time doomsday prognosticators to crawl out from under every rock to spread disinformation and propaganda.

People were predicting the end of the world. Individuals who misapplied terminology disseminated erroneous information concerning the mark of the beast found in the Book of Revelation. These deceivers claimed the mark of the beast would be administered to those receiving vaccinations for the Coronavirus. Due to their lack of knowledge, many uninformed believers did not know how to refute this bogus information. Pastors and other church leaders were carried away in this falsehood and ended up spreading this error.

It is amazing how quickly people embrace foolishness. You would be surprised that if you asked the average Christian what are the signs of the end times or what is the rapture, and where in the Bible is this event documented, they wouldn't know. Even if you asked where in the Scriptures does it talk about the Antichrist, once again people would draw a blank.

This begs the question, why are so many people ignorant of what the Bible teaches about the end times? Let's examine a few reasons. The first reason pastors and laypersons alike avoid teaching eschatology is because there are many opposing views and different systems of interpretation. Not only is the subject difficult, but all the divergent views make it confusing and hard to untangle. Still others have apprehensions about the symbology, metaphors, and the images contained in the Book of Revelation—they are put off or hesitant to try to make sense of it. Then others believe doctrines that tell Christians that most of Revelation does not apply to the Church, so there is no need to bother with it. Still other ministers have not taken the time to study this subject and therefore do not teach it because of their own knowledge deficit.

Whatever reason people do not engage in end time prophecy only exposes a deeper problem. The real issue is the ignorance. People focus on other aspects of the Word of God to the neglect of subjects related to final things. What the Scriptures reveal concerning the events that are coming on this world are important and can inform the decisions we make. If a person believes the Coronavirus vaccine contains the mark of the beast, making a medical decision based on that information could prove to be detrimental. Therefore, having at least a basic knowledge of end time subjects will help keep you grounded, as bad information seeks to exploit and mislead those who are uninformed.

Therefore, this book is not designed to promote a particular eschatological position, but to educate people who have little knowledge about end time prophecy. Even a basic knowledge will be helpful in defending against erroneous information that could lead people astray.

Though the content in this book is primarily cursory, the reader will walk away after reading this book with a working knowledge of end time prophecy. The author has avoided drawing the reader into lengthy essays. Each chapter is written in non-technical terms so that the average Christian can read and understand it. It is the author's express intent to keep this material accessible so that all may benefit from this work, because it is vital that *you must know the times*.

My people are destroyed for lack of knowledge... Hosea 4:6

1

THE SIGNS OF THE TIMES

"But He replied to them, "When it is evening, you say, 'It will be fair weather, for the sky is red.' "And in the morning, 'There will be a storm today, for the sky is red and threatening.' Do you know how to discern the appearance of the sky, but cannot the discern signs of the times?"
Matthew 16:2-3

What are the signs of the times, is a question that has sparked an endless debate among scholars and laypersons alike. In the Gospels, the disciples asked Jesus, "Tell us, when will these things happen, and what *will be* the sign of Your coming, and of the end of the age" (Mt. 24:3). Additionally, the saints at the church of Thessalonica, and those to whom John addressed in his First Epistle, were very interested in learning more about the end times and specifically about the Antichrist (2 Thes. 2:1-2, 1 John 2:18). Today, in the twenty-first century, people are still asking the same questions.

Though there is much we do not know concerning how prophetic events will unfold, what we do know is what is recorded in the Scriptures. Therefore, no signs given in the Bible are to be ignored. If the Bible gives a sign, pay attention to it. All believers were admonished "to watch as well as pray" (Mark 13:32). However, you cannot watch if you do not know what the Bible teaches what to look out for. In the following passage, Jesus described what the world would be like when he returns.

And just as it happened in the **days of Noah,** so it will be also in the days of the Son of Man: they were eating, they were drinking, they were marrying, they were being given in marriage, until the day that Noah entered the ark, and the flood came and destroyed them all. "It was the same as happened in the **days of Lot:** they were eating, they were drinking, they were buying, they were selling, they were planting, they were building; but on the day that Lot went out from **Sodom** it rained fire and brimstone from heaven and destroyed them all. "It will be just the same on the day that the Son of Man is revealed. Luke 17:26-30

The question is, what were the days of Noah and Sodom and Gomorrah like? Here is what we know about Noah's days.

Then the LORD saw that the wickedness of man was great on the earth, and that every intent of the thoughts of his heart was only evil continually. Genesis 6:5

There are many deep philosophical and theological issues that the flood narrative presents that go far beyond the scope of this study. However, the point here is that wickedness caused the human race to degrade to such a degree that it was necessary to "reset" or start over again. How God chose to do this was destruction through the flood, leaving only Noah's family alive to replenish the world. It is important to understand that the purpose of this ancient text is not to answer all the questions to the satisfaction of a twenty-first century individual's inquiry. However, the point at hand is how morally debased humanity had become. What this tells us is that moral decay will be thematic and prevalent before the Lord returns. Things that are right will be declared to be wrong. What is wrong will be declared as good and right. It is one thing to sin and know it's wrong, but it's another thing altogether for sin to be called righteousness.

Isaiah declares,

Woe to those who call evil good and good evil, who put darkness for light and light for darkness, who put bitter for sweet and sweet for bitter. Woe to those who are wise in their own eyes and clever in their own sight. Woe to those who are heroes at drinking wine and champions at mixing drinks, who acquit the guilty for a bribe, but deny justice to the innocent. Isaiah 5:20-23, NIV

During the times preceding the coming of the Lord, the world will be topsy-turvy, where darkness will be the light in people's eyes. Jesus speaks of this condition when he states,

> The eye is the lamp of the body; so then if your eye is clear, your whole body will be full of light. "But if your eye is bad, your whole body will be full of darkness. If then the light that is in you is darkness, how great is the darkness! Matthew 6:22-23

The common metaphor for wickedness throughout the Bible is *darkness*. The interesting aspect about this truth is that for people who are unregenerate or not saved, their light is actually darkness. Therefore, they cannot know or perceive things pertaining to the kingdom of God, nor receive the glorious light of Jesus Christ. Spiritual blindness is also another metaphor for that which is used in the Scripture for people in darkness. The apostle Paul declares,

> And even if our gospel is veiled, it is veiled to those who are perishing, in whose case the god of this world has blinded the minds of the unbelieving so that they might not see the light of the gospel of the glory of Christ, who is the image of God. 2 Corinthians 4:3-4

Jesus also spoke of the world being like Sodom and Gomorrah. The question is, What was that like? Unrestrained sexual perversion both heterosexual and homosexual, but particularly homosexual. The text reads,

> Before they had gone to bed, all the men from every part of the city of Sodom—both young and old—surrounded the house. They called to Lot, "Where are the men who came to you tonight? Bring them out to us so that we can have sex with them." Lot went outside to meet them and shut the door behind him and said, "No, my friends. Don't do this wicked thing (Genesis 19:4-7, NIV).

It is interesting that Lot pleads with them not to do this "wicked thing." Attempting to reason with them, he offered his daughters as an attempt to distract them from wanting to have sex with these angels whom the mob believed to be normal human beings. However, the men were so filled with vile, inordinate lust that they were not distracted, but threatened to do even worse to Lot. Amazingly, after the angels struck the mob blind, they still groped in the dark trying to find the door to get to the angels.

Jude also echoes the wickedness of these people when he writes,

> In a similar way, Sodom and Gomorrah and the surrounding towns gave themselves up to sexual immorality and perversion. They serve as an example of those who suffer the punishment of eternal fire. Jude 7, NIV

In an attempt to mitigate the impact that these passages have in making the case against wicked lifestyles, many claim that homosexuality was not the real issue, but it was the fact that it was the intent of the men to perpetrate a violent mob rape on innocent visitors to the city. However, that response is inadequate, because judgment for Sodom's wickedness had already been pronounced before the angels arrived and the mob reacted. Abraham actually pleaded with God not to destroy the city because the righteous would also perish (Gen.18:16-33, 19:1-29). Therefore, the days of Noah and Sodom and Gomorrah is the template the Lord chose to use to convey how the last days would be. The question is, do we see these things in our world today? I think the answer is obvious.

In Paul's second letter to Timothy, the apostle warns,

> But mark this: There will be terrible times in the last days. People will be lovers of themselves, lovers of money, boastful, proud, abusive, disobedient to their parents, ungrateful, unholy, without love, unforgiving, slanderous, without self-control, brutal, not lovers of the good, treacherous, rash, conceited, lovers of pleasure rather than lovers of God—having a form of godliness but denying its power. Have nothing to do with such people. They are the kind who worm their way into homes and gain control over gullible women, who are loaded down with sins and are swayed by all kinds of evil desires, always learning but never able to come to a knowledge of the truth. 2 Timothy 3:1-7, NIV

The world will be in darkness. People will get worse and worse (2 Tim. 3:13). As a whole, things are not going to get better. Iniquity will increase, causing the love of many to grow cold (Mt. 24:12). Yet, people will be going about their daily lives not being able to discern the times. They will think everything is normal. They will claim "peace and safety" (1 Thes. 5:3). They will also mock those who expect the Lord to return. Peter observes the following.

> Above all, you must understand that in the last days scoffers will come, scoffing, and following their own evil desires. They will say, "Where is this 'coming' he promised? Ever since our ancestors died, everything goes on as it has since the beginning of creation."
>
> 2 Peter 3:3-4, NIV

The world will start to openly mock foundational Christian beliefs such as the rapture. Expect to see more laws passed restricting the rights of Christians to express their faith. Persecution is a part of being a Christian. More attacks against the Christians in America and elsewhere will occur (2 Tim. 3:12).

There will be…fearful events and great signs from heaven (Luke 21:11, NIV). For example, in Revelation 8, a flaming star called wormwood hits the earth and poisons the water (Rev. 8:10-11). Interestingly, the word for "star" comes from the Greek word *aster*, from which we get the English word asteroid. When meteorites enter the Earth's atmosphere, they are set ablaze due to atmospheric friction. These are examples of fearful sightings in the heavens.

Remember the meteor that exploded over the Russian city of Chelyabinsk in 2013? Experts said that it was a small asteroid about the size of a six-story building. The energy released from this blast was equivalent to a nuclear explosion. The damage on the ground was extensive.

Secondly, though I am not advocating for the reality of extraterrestrial beings and flying saucers, fearful sightings in the heavens are part of the end-time prophecy landscape. Luke's account is explicit: "men's hearts failing them from fear and the expectation of those things which are coming on the earth, for the powers of heaven will be shaken" (Luke 21:26, NKJV). Whatever this means, or however it plays out in real time, people will faint and suffer heart attacks when great signs from heaven appear.

The rise of false prophets and false doctrines will manifest in churches throughout the world. Those who are big on seeking signs and wonders will be prime candidates for deception. Jesus warned,

> For false messiahs and false prophets will appear and perform great signs and wonders to deceive, if possible, even the elect. See, I have told you ahead of time. "So if anyone tells you, 'There he is, out in the wilderness,' do not go out; or, 'Here he is, in the inner rooms,' do not believe it. Matthew 24:24-26, NIV

False prophets can only thrive in churches that do not teach sound doctrine; therefore, the apostle warns,

> For the time will come when people will not put up with sound doctrine. Instead, to suit their own desires, they will gather around them a great number of teachers to say what their itching ears want to hear. They will turn their ears away from the truth and turn aside to myths. 2 Timothy 4:3-4, NIV

This passage informs us that instead of sound doctrine, people would opt for myths, which in the Greek means speech, conversation, also of narrative or story without distinction of fact or fiction. False prophets and ministers seek to dazzle people with unverifiable tall tells of miracles, supernatural manifestations, and power. Gullible carnal Christians prefer this type of junk food teaching and preaching because it appeals to the emotions and feels good, brings no conviction of sin, but dilutes the gospel message with promises of wealth, prosperity, and cessation of life's difficulties. The pursuit of wealth and materialism is one of the most powerful distractions the world uses to keep people blind and insensitive to what is really happening. While being seduced by what the world has to offer, you cannot pay attention to the signs of the times. In Romans Paul warns,

> Do this, knowing the time, that it is already the hour for you to awaken from sleep; for now salvation is nearer to us than when we believed. The night is almost gone, and the day is near. Therefore, let us lay aside the deeds of darkness and put on the armor of light. Let us behave properly as in the day, not in carousing and drunkenness, not in sexual promiscuity and sensuality, not in strife and jealousy. But put on the Lord Jesus Christ, and make no provision for the flesh in regard to its lusts. Romans 13:11-14

2

What is Eschatology?

According to the *Webster's Online Dictionary*, eschatology is defined as the "branch of theology concerned with the final events in the history of the world or of humankind." It comes from the Greek *eschatos*, which means "last or farthest." Specifically, the study of eschatology encompasses the whole body of subjects that focus on the last things, such as: the Second Advent (or return) of Christ, the rapture of the Church, the resurrection of the just and the unrighteous, all of the events concerning the tribulation period, the Day of the Lord, the rise of the Antichrist and false prophet, the mark of the beast, the Battle of Armageddon, the binding of Satan, the Millennial reign of Christ, the final judgment of the wicked, the new heaven and earth, and many other associated topics concerning the end of the world, and the ushering in of the eternal age.

The greatest concentration of eschatological material is found in the Book of Revelation. However, other New Testament books that have this material are Matthew 24-25, Mark 13, Luke 21, Romans 8-11, 1 Cor. 15, 1 Thessalonians 4 and 5, 2 Thessalonians 2, 2 Peter 2-3, and Jude. Other New Testament epistles also speak of the end times, such as 2 Tim 3:1, Titus 2:13, and 1 John 2:18. However, this is not an exhaustive list of Scriptures that deal with eschatological studies. Old Testament prophets such as Daniel and Ezekiel have the most eschatological material, with Isaiah, Jeremiah, Obadiah, Joel, Zechariah, and Zephaniah all containing some "last days" writings.

Eschatological writings would fall under the Bible genre called *apocalyptic literature*. Apocalyptic means *making fully known, revelation, disclosure*. Its focus is predicting imminent disaster and total or universal destruction. The term is also used in a general sense. Disasters are often characterized as being "apocalyptic." Apocalyptic literature typically features frightening symbols, and bizarre imagery, metaphors, personifications, and hyperboles. Some also refer to the imagery of Revelation as "verbal cartoons," where aspects of Israel's historical conflict with Satan is displayed as a *woman clothed with the sun, with the moon under her feet, and on her head a garland of twelve stars that gives birth to* a *man child* (Christ) and is pursued by a *red dragon with seven heads and ten horns…*" (Satan).

Other prominent characters of apocalyptic literature are angels who execute God's plan. In Revelation angels blow the seven trumpets, pour out God's wrath in the seven bowl judgments, and carry out many functionary roles, including unveiling mysteries. In Daniel, the archangels Michael and Gabriel are both prominent characters as the guardian over the nation of Israel and revealer of prophetic revelation.

Care must be taken in attempting to interpret apocalyptic literature. Due to its cryptic nature, tight doctrinal boundaries should not be drawn around apocalyptic literature alone. To avoid confusion, interpretation should be consistent with other eschatological material and subjects found throughout the Scriptures. For example, material found in the Book of Revelation is consistent with Isaiah, Jeremiah, Daniel, Ezekiel, Zechariah, and other Old Testament prophets.

Though there are many prevailing interpretations of the Book of Revelation and eschatology in general, this subject should be approached with humility, because we have not reached the end yet. Much is yet to be fulfilled. Therefore, no one person or doctrinal interpretation has all the answers. Just as people struggled to understand all the associated prophecies concerning the first coming of the Lord, so are there still many unknowns concerning His second coming. God *has not* revealed everything. For example, when the seven thunders of Rev. 10:4 spoke their revelation, John was specifically forbidden to write it down. God intentionally made it known that He prevented this information from being disclosed.

Furthermore, what He has revealed, no one is sure how He will bring it to pass. We know the *what* of prophecy, but the *how* and *when* of prophecy no man knows for sure. For example, Micah 5:2 prophesied that Jesus would be born in Bethlehem. However, no one knew when that would happen, nor could they have predicted that a tax and census decreed by Augustus Caesar would be the reason why both Mary and Joseph would be in Bethlehem (see Luke 2:1-7).

Since God can use anything or anyone in all creation to fulfill His prophetic word, this makes knowing how God will bring prophecy to pass inaccessible to humans until it is fulfilled. There is simply no way a human being can calculate how God is going to do something unless God reveals it. *His ways are past finding out* (Rom. 11:33).

Information concerning the end of the world and doomsday scenarios have been a favorite of the film industry, enthusiast and conspiracist alike. Due to all the mystery associated with apocalyptic literature, people tend to gravitate to it because their interest is piqued. Unfortunately, there have been many doomsday cults like the *Branch Davidians* that have risen based upon heretical interpretations of Revelation and other end time prophecies found in the Bible. On the other hand, Christians can overemphasize dogmatic positions even to the point of disfellowshipping and ridiculing those who believe differently. This is why it is important to understand—no matter what position one embraces—that no one but God has all the answers.

3

ARE THESE THE LAST DAYS?

The *Last Days* is a subject that falls under the general heading of eschatology. In the Old Testament the term is found in Deuteronomy 4:30, "When thou art in tribulation, and all these things are come upon thee, *even* in the latter days, if thou turn to the LORD thy God, and shalt be obedient unto his voice." Isaiah says, "And it shall come to pass in the last days, *that* the mountain of the LORD'S house shall be established in the top of the mountains, and shall be exalted above the hills; and all nations shall flow unto it" (Isaiah 2:2, KJV). And in Micah 4:1-3, which is almost identical to Isaiah's prophecy, both speak of the Lord's Messianic Kingdom in the last days, that will be established after the Lord's return to the earth during His Millennial reign (more on this later).

On the day of Pentecost, Peter began his powerful sermon with the following words, "And it shall come to pass in the *last days*, saith God, I will pour out of my Spirit upon all flesh" (Acts 2:17). These words, and the verses that follow, were quotes from the prophet Joel (see Joel 2:28-33) that prophesied about the birth of the Church. The notable aspect of the prophecy is that the term *last days* has been in application for 2,000 years now. Therefore, in this context, *the last days* encompass the entire span of the Church age from Pentecost to the rapture.

The synonymous terms "latter years" or "latter days" are found in the Old Testament thirteen times. For example, in Daniel the term is used as follows, "Now I have come to give you an understanding of what will happen to your people in the *latter days*, for the vision pertains to the days yet *future*" (Daniel 10:14). Speaking of Israel being back in their land, Ezekiel also uses the term,

After many days thou shalt be visited: *in the latter years* thou shalt come into the land *that is* brought back from the sword, *and is* gathered out of many people, against the mountains of Israel, which have been always waste: but it is brought forth out of the nations, and they shall dwell safely all of them. Ezek. 38:8-9

Once again, we see a clear eschatological connection. This prophecy speaks of Israel being reformed as a nation that was to occur in *the latter years,* which happened on May 14, 1948. Therefore, this clearly puts the times that we live now in *the last days.* Someone born in 1948 would be 72 in 2020, well within a typical lifespan.

In the New Testament, the term is both singular and plural. The singular "last day" is used five times (John 6:39,40, 44,54; 11:24) by Jesus in reference to the resurrection of the righteous, and once speaking of the judgment of the unrighteous (12:48).

In 1 Timothy 4:1, a variant is used, "But the Spirit explicitly says that in *later times* some will fall away from the faith, paying attention to deceitful spirits and doctrines of demons."

In 2 Timothy, Paul, speaking of the future, describes the last days.

But know this, that in the last days perilous times will come: For men will be lovers of themselves, lovers of money, boasters, proud, blasphemers, disobedient to parents, unthankful, unholy, unloving, unforgiving, slanderers, without self-control, brutal, despisers of good, traitors, headstrong, haughty, lovers of pleasure rather than lovers of God, having a form of godliness but denying its power. And from such people turn away! 2 Timothy 3:1-7, NKJV

The litany of vices in this verse certainly characterizes the times that we live in now. Sin, debauchery, and lasciviousness are portrayed through the media, movies, and music as the right way to live. The fact that Paul said, "perilous times shall come…" indicates that he wasn't only speaking of his current times, but a time in the future before the return of the Lord.

These sinful manifestations shall bring judgment on the world. James 5:3 speaks of the judgment of the unrighteous in the "last days." Peter and Jude (vs. 18 *last time*) also speak of the scoffers and mockers that will come in the last days, ridiculing those who patiently wait for the coming of the Lord (2 Peter 3:3).

From these verses we understand that the term "last days" can have a wide application that covers the span of Church history, or it could be more focused on the end times. As it relates to the eschatological end times, these days are characterized by "perilous times," full of social and political unrest, inspired by people who are getting increasingly worse because they are being inspired by demonic activity. However, in the last days, there will be a *specific day* where the Lord returns in glory to set up His kingdom here on the earth.

This is the promise that we have who love His appearing and patiently wait for His return. So, with all of this, there is good news. As Luke states in his Gospel, "But when these things begin to take place, straighten up and lift up your heads, because your redemption is drawing near." Then He told them a parable: "Behold the fig tree and all the trees; as soon as they put forth *leaves,* you see it and know for yourselves that summer is now near. "So you also, when you see these things happening, recognize that the kingdom of God is near. Luke 21:28-31. Truly these are the *last days*.

4

WHAT IS THE DAY OF THE LORD?

In an eschatological sense, *the Day of the Lord* is a period where God pours out his wrath on the world. In general, it is not a literal twenty-four-hour day, although there will be a specific *day* when the Lord literally returns to initiate His earthly kingdom. Therefore, the Day of the Lord can be seen as both a period of time and a specific day. Characteristically, "That day will be a great and terrible day, a day of darkness and gloominess, a day of the vengeance of God. While some of these prophetic utterances may have referred to the judgment of God in history, their ultimate fulfillment will come in a final act by which the world and its inhabitants will give account to God" (Holman Bible Dictionary).

In Isaiah 13, the Day of the Lord speaks of the destruction of Babylon but also has a broader futuristic application that is eschatological. Though there are many Old Testament passages that speak of the Day of the Lord, some are given below.

Behold, the day of the LORD comes, Cruel, with both wrath and fierce anger, To lay the land desolate; And He will destroy its sinners from it. For the stars of heaven and their constellations Will not give their light; The sun will be darkened in its going forth, And the moon will not cause its light to shine. "I will punish the world for *its* evil, And the wicked for their iniquity; I will halt the arrogance of the proud, And will lay low the haughtiness of the terrible. Isaiah 13:9-11, NKJV

The great day of the LORD *is* near; *It is* near and hastens quickly. The noise of the day of the LORD is bitter; There the mighty men shall cry out. That day *is* a day of wrath, A day of trouble and distress, A day of devastation and desolation, A day of darkness and gloominess, A day of clouds and thick darkness. Zephaniah 1:14-15, NKJV

Behold, the day of the LORD is coming, And your spoil will be divided in your midst. For I will gather all the nations to battle against Jerusalem; The city shall be taken, The houses rifled, And the women ravished. Half of the city shall go into captivity, But the remnant of the people shall not be cut off from the city. Zechariah 14:1-2, NKJV

Then you shall flee *through* My mountain valley, For the mountain valley shall reach to Azal. Yes, you shall flee As you fled from the earthquake In the days of Uzziah king of Judah. Thus the LORD my God will come, *And* all the saints with You. It shall come to pass in that day *That* there will be no light; The lights will diminish. It shall be one day Which is known to the LORD—Neither day nor night. But at evening time it shall happen *That* it will be light. Zechariah 14:5-7, NKJV

From these passages we can conclude the following: 1) The Day of the Lord is yet future. 2) The Day of the Lord is a time of God's wrath being poured out where He punishes the world. 3) It is also the time where the nation of Israel goes through judgment as characterized in Jeremiah 30:7, *the time of Jacob's trouble* and as also seen in Zech. 14:1-2. 4) The tribulations and upheavals experienced during this time culminate with the Lord's return as *King of Kings and Lord of Lords*, accompanied with His saints during the battle of Armageddon. The Lord's invasion from heaven is also depicted in Revelation.

Now I saw heaven opened, and behold, a white horse. And He who sat on him *was* called Faithful and True, and in righteousness He judges and makes war. His eyes *were* like a flame of fire, and on His head *were* many crowns. He had a name written that no one knew except Himself. He *was* clothed with a robe dipped in blood, and His name is called The Word of God. And the armies in heaven, clothed in fine linen, white and clean, followed Him on white horses. Now out of His mouth goes a sharp sword, that with it He should strike the nations. And He Himself will rule them with a rod of iron. He Himself treads the winepress of the fierceness and wrath of Almighty God. Revelation 19:11-15, NKJV

In 2 Thessalonians 2, the Apostle Paul also writes of the times that encompass the Day of the Lord.

...and to *give* you who are troubled rest with us when the Lord Jesus is revealed from heaven with His mighty angels, in flaming fire taking vengeance on those who do not know God, and on those who do not obey the gospel of our Lord Jesus Christ. These shall be punished with everlasting destruction from the presence of the Lord and from the glory of His power, when He comes, in that Day, to be glorified in His saints and to be admired among all those who believe, because our testimony among you was believed.

2 Thessalonians 1:7-10, NKJV

THE COSMIC SIGNS

The cosmic signs (celestial events in the heavens) are closely associated with the *Day of the Lord,* and appear *before* and throughout the period. Joel's prophecy concerning this event is important. "The sun shall be turned into darkness, And the moon into blood, *before* the coming of the great and awesome day of the LORD" Joel 2:31 (NKJV). In his powerful sermon on the *Day of Pentecost,* Peter quotes from Joel's prophecy, echoing the same truth about the cosmological signs preceding the coming of the Day of the Lord (see Acts 2:20).

In the Gospels, Jesus also speaks of the cosmic signs.

Immediately after the tribulation of those days the sun will be darkened, and the moon will not give its light; the stars will fall from heaven, and the powers of the heavens will be shaken.

Matthew 24:29, NKJV

And there will be signs in the sun, in the moon, and in the stars; and on the earth distress of nations, with perplexity, the sea and the waves roaring; Luke 21:25, NKJV

In Revelation, John also speaks of these heavenly signs.

> I looked when He opened the sixth seal, and behold, there was a great earthquake; and the sun became black as sackcloth of hair, and the moon became like blood. And the stars of heaven fell to the earth, as a fig tree drops its late figs when it is shaken by a mighty wind... For the great day of His wrath has come, and who is able to stand?"
> Rev. 6:12-13, 17, NKJV

All these prophecies speak of the *cosmic signs*. The important thing to remember is that they appear *before* the Day of the Lord comes.

The Great Tribulation

The *Day of the Lord* shall be a unique period in the history of the world. There has not been anything like it before, and there will be nothing like it after it. There shall be unparalleled distress upon humankind, the nations, the ecology, and global upheaval from the heavens above, unequalled seismic activity beneath, and terrifying supernatural and demonic activity shall torment the inhabitants of the world. Of this time, Jesus specifically stated,

> For then there will be great tribulation, *such as has not been since the beginning of the world until this time, no, nor ever shall be.* And unless those days were shortened, no flesh would be saved; but for the elect's sake those days will be shortened. Matthew 24:21-22, NKJV

From the unequalled time depicted in this text, we get the term "The great tribulation." Daniel also speaks of this time in his prophecy.

> At that time Michael shall stand up, The great prince who stands *watch* over the sons of your people; *And there shall be a time of trouble, Such as never was since there was a nation, Even to that time.* And at that time your people shall be delivered, Every one who is found written in the book. Daniel 12:1, NKJV

Paul gives Christians some important assurances about this unique time. In 1 Thessalonians 5 the apostle writes,

But concerning the times and the seasons, brethren, you have no need that I should write to you. For you yourselves know perfectly that the *day of the Lord* so comes as a thief in the night. For when they say, "Peace and safety!" then sudden destruction comes upon them, as labor pains upon a pregnant woman. And they shall not escape. But you, brethren, are not in darkness, so that this Day should overtake you as a thief. You are all sons of light and sons of the day. We are not of the night nor of darkness...For God did not appoint us to wrath, but to obtain salvation through our Lord Jesus Christ. 1 Thessalonians 5:1-5, 9 NKJV

Here Paul's focus is primarily on the events that will occur during the great tribulation before the Lord's Second Advent (second coming), where Jesus returns to start his reign during the Millennium. However, Paul clearly assures all Christians that God has not appointed the Church to the Day of the Lord, the time of God's wrath. Paul also speaks of the time when the world will be saying "peace and safety" how sudden destruction will seize the world. Many believe that the peace and safety that Paul is alluding to will come as a result of peace in the Middle East, between Israel and her surrounding, once-hostile neighbors. This peace can also be a brief time of world peace ushered in by the Antichrist, who during the first half of the final seven years will be a man of peace. However, he will become the beast of Revelation 13 (more on this later).

Peter expands the Day of the Lord concept to include the new heaven and new earth.

But the day of the Lord will come as a thief in the night, in which the heavens will pass away with a great noise, and the elements will melt with fervent heat; both the earth and the works that are in it will be burned up. Therefore, since all these things will be dissolved, what manner *of persons* ought you to be in holy conduct and godliness, looking for and hastening the coming of the day of God, because of which the heavens will be dissolved, being on fire, and the elements will melt with fervent heat? Nevertheless we, according to His promise, look for new heavens and a new earth in which righteousness dwells. 2 Peter 3:10-13, NKJV

Drawn from Old Testament text found in Isa. 65:17 and 66:22, Peter also places the new heaven and new earth under the heading of the *Day of the Lord.* Therefore, in its fullest sense, the Day of the Lord includes the last eschatological act before entering the eternal age, the creation of the new heaven and earth. In Revelation, John picks up this theme when he writes, "Now I saw a new heaven and a new earth, for the first heaven and the first earth had passed away..." (Revelation 21:1, NKJV).

Therefore, *the Day of the Lord* is a period of time where the Lord pours out His wrath on the earth, where all the wickedness of the nations and people will be brought into judgment by an angry God. The Day of the Lord is also synonymous with the wrath of God. In 1 Thes. 5:9, Paul declares that the Church is not appointed to the wrath of God. Vivid imagery of this terrible time can be seen in the Book of Revelation, which speaks of various judgments that climax with the Lord's return to fight in the Battle of Armageddon. Therefore, the Day of the Lord is the period in which God pours out his wrath on the earth. It culminates with the day the Lord actually returns in glory to begin His reign on earth, and finally it is the creation of the new heaven and new earth.

5

WHAT DID JESUS SAY ABOUT THE
END OF THE AGE?

The Mount Olivet Discourse

According to the *New Unger's Bible Dictionary,* The Mount of Olives is a limestone ridge that is about a mile in length, running in a north-south direction covering the whole eastern side of the city of Jerusalem. It was there where the Lord answered the disciples' questions concerning the end of the world (age). In Matthew 24:1-59, Mark 13:1-37, and Luke 21:5-36 is contained the discussion called *the Mount Olivet Discourse.* Within the context of these gospel narratives Jesus disclosed details about future events concerning the destruction of the temple and Jerusalem that would come to pass in 70 A.D., and eschatological events that would precede his return as King of King and Lord of Lords.

> Jesus answered: "Watch out that no one deceives you. For many will come in my name, claiming, 'I am the Messiah,' and will deceive many. You will hear of wars and rumors of wars, but see to it that you are not alarmed. Such things must happen, but the end is still to come. Nation will rise against nation, and kingdom against kingdom. There will be famines and earthquakes in various places. All these are the beginning of birth pains. "Then you will be handed over to be persecuted and put to death, and you will be hated by all nations because of me. At that time many will turn away from the faith and will betray and hate each other....Matthew 24:4-10, NIV

It is interesting that the Lord describes the signs of the end of the age (or end of the world, KJV) as being "birth pains." This analogy describes the level of intensity and frequency of events that will increase as the end approaches, just as a woman's birth pains increase in frequency and intensity as her delivery date comes. We can categorize the signs of the end as follows:

Verses 4-5, *False prophets and false christs*

speak of *times of deception* caused by pseudo-messiahs and false prophets will arise; some even claiming to be the Messiah himself. These false prophets will have power to perform signs and wonders and will deceive many (vs.24).

Verse 6, *Wars and rumors of wars*

indicate conflicts and wars between nations, but more specifically, the rumors of wars are what fueled the arms races between nations such as Russia and the United States. One side makes weapons to counter the other side's weapons. This includes nuclear arms development, strategic bombers, missile defense systems, and outer space defense technology on the basis of "just in case," in order to keep pace with the enemy, fueled by propaganda or political agendas. Another important prophetic insight is the prophecy says *nation shall rise against nation*. The word *nation* comes from the Greek word *ethnos*, where we get our English word *ethnicity*. Therefore, tensions between ethnic groups around the world will also be characteristic of those times. America is a prime example of how racial tensions can reach dangerous flash points leading to alarming social unrest.

Verse 7, *Famines and earthquakes in various places*

speak of the increasing intensity and frequency of natural disasters. Luke's gospel (21:11, 25-26) expands this list and adds *pestilences* and *fearful sights* and *great signs* shall there be from heaven. Luke also includes cosmic signs, "And there will be signs in the sun, in the moon, and in the stars; and on the earth distress of nations, with perplexity, the sea and the waves roaring; men's hearts failing them from fear and the expectation of those things which are coming on the earth, for the powers of heaven will be shaken" (Luke 21:25-26, NKJV, see Mt. 24:29). It is interesting that the *roaring waves* prediction would also include destruction from tsunamis as seen in the Indian Ocean in 2004, and the devastating tsunami that destroyed coastal cities of Japan in 2011.

In 2021, extreme weather has been wreaking havoc all over the world. Overwhelming floods, tornados, and hurricanes have devastated several cities in America, Germany, China, Turkey, and India as well as wildfires that have scorched millions of acres in America, Australia, Greece, and other nations. In August 2021, another catastrophic earthquake struck Haiti killing thousands. All these are a few examples of the intensifying birth pangs.

Verse 10, *Persecution, and defection from the faith*

"Then you will be handed over to be persecuted and put to death, and you will be hated by all nations because of me. At that time many will turn away from the faith and will betray and hate each other (Mt. 24:9-10, NIV). Here in Matthew, Jesus forewarns of a time where believers under threat of death will abandon the faith. Paul also speaks of a *falling away*, before the Day of the Lord comes (2 Thes. 2:3); more on this later.

Persecution is something that modern-day Christians in the West are not very familiar. Especially in America, Christians tend to believe that they are immune to being persecuted. This is largely because of the religious freedoms that are granted by the U.S. Constitution. Additionally, in our churches believers are not taught to expect it. However, as the end approaches, religious freedom will come under attack. Christians will bear the ire of a Christ-hating world, because of their faithfulness to Jesus Christ and their refusal to compromise with the world (also see 2 Tim. 3:12-13). It is during these times that things will be turned upside down. Right will be wrong. Wrong will be right. Light will be seen as darkness and darkness seen as light (Isa. 5:20). This is the result when there is an assault on the truth. Truth cannot be easily distinguished, where lies and disinformation dominate the political, social, legal, and religious narratives. Where deceit persists confusion and lawlessness will thrive.

Verse 15, *The Abomination of Desolation*

is one of the more prominent and pivotal eschatological signs in the Bible. The following chapter will be dedicated to this subject.

Verses 36-41, *As it was in the days of Noah*

"But about that day or hour no one knows, not even the angels in heaven, nor the Son, but only the Father. As it was in the days of Noah, so it will be at the coming of the Son of Man. For in the days before the flood, people were eating and drinking, marrying and giving in marriage, up to the day Noah entered the ark; and they knew nothing about what would happen until the flood came and took them all away. That is how it will be at the coming of the Son of Man. Two men will be in the field; one will be taken and the other left. Two women will be grinding with a hand mill; one will be taken and the other left. (NIV 2011)

A few important points can be taken from these verses.

1) *No one knows the day or the hour of the Lord's return.* Even though there have been many who have supposedly calculated the day of the Lord's return, they have been wrong one hundred percent of the time. If Jesus doesn't know, it seems to be quite insane to think someone else could know. Though it is perplexing how Jesus who is omniscient does not know something, it's probably not that complicated. The Lord could exercise His divine prerogative not to know this information (see Heb. 8:12, 10:17). But no matter how we attempt to solve how the Lord doesn't know something, this we can know, to avoid anyone who claims that they know the day the Lord is returning.

2) The time prior to Jesus' return is characterized as *being as the days of Noah.* The Scriptures teach that "...*the wickedness of man was great in the earth, and that every intent of the thoughts of his heart was only evil continually*" (Gen. 6.5, NKJV). Therefore, God in His wrath responded to man's iniquity by sending the flood. Just as they were in Noah's day, wicked people carried on in their daily activities, unaware of pending doom, until the flood came.

Luke's gospel adds another layer to understanding these days when he writes, "Likewise as it was also in the days of Lot: They ate, they drank, they bought, they sold, they planted, they built; but on the day that Lot went out of Sodom it rained fire and brimstone from heaven and destroyed *them* all" Luke 17:28-29 (NKJV).

Therefore, the conditions in the world before the Lord's return can be characterized by ancient biblical judgment events, as the *days of Noah* and *Sodom and Gomorrah.*

Verses 40-42, *One will be taken and the other left*

"Then two *men* will be in the field: one will be taken and the other left. Two *women will be* grinding at the mill: one will be taken and the other left. Watch therefore, for you do not know what hour your Lord is coming" (NKJV).

Many believe that this passage is referring to the rapture (more about the rapture later). However, Luke gives more information that will help us correctly understand this passage.

Jesus' answer is telling. After being told about people being taken, the disciples wanted to know where they would be taken. Jesus answered, "Where the body *is,* there also the vultures will be gathered." Luke 17:36-37

The word *body* in this passage comes from the Greek word *soma.* One of the definitions for this word is "a corpse." Therefore, the NIV translates it this way,

"Where, Lord?" they asked. He replied, "Where there is a dead body, there the vultures will gather."

From Luke's gospel we can understand that this passage is not about the rapture. So, what is it about? After the battle of Armageddon is over, where the Lord has slain the gathering armies in the plain of Megiddo, He sends an angel to call for the birds to devour the corpses that have fallen in battle. The Book of Revelation gives a clear picture of this great feast prepared for the birds.

> Then I saw an angel standing in the sun; and he cried with a loud voice, saying to all the birds that fly in the midst of heaven, "Come and gather together for the supper of the great God, that you may eat the flesh of kings, the flesh of captains, the flesh of mighty men, the flesh of horses and of those who sit on them, and the flesh of

all *people*, free and slave, both small and great."... And the rest were killed with the sword which proceeded from the mouth of Him who sat on the horse. And all the birds were filled with their flesh.

Rev. 19:17-18, 21; also see Ezek. 39:17-19

This passage looks forward to the culminating eschatological event of this age, where the cleanup after the slaughter of Armageddon is initiated. The fowls of the air are the first guests invited to this apocalyptic banquet where the corpses of soldiers from the world's armies will be the main course.

The final aspect of the Olivet Discourse that I will cover in this chapter is found only in Luke's account. "But when you see Jerusalem surrounded by armies, then know that its desolation is near... And they will fall by the edge of the sword and be led away captive into all nations. And Jerusalem will be trampled by Gentiles until the times of the Gentiles are fulfilled (Luke 21:20, 24 NKJV).

Many scholars agree that this reference, and the information that follows in verses 21-23, is about the fall of Jerusalem in 70 A.D. However, that being the case, there is still a future fulfillment that calls for Jerusalem to be surrounded by armies that occurs during the Day of the Lord, right before Christ returns.

Behold, the day of the LORD is coming, And your spoil will be divided in your midst. For I will gather all the nations to battle against Jerusalem; The city shall be taken, The houses rifled, And the women ravished. Half of the city shall go into captivity, But the remnant of the people shall not be cut off from the city. Then the LORD will go forth And fight against those nations, As He fights in the day of battle. Zechariah 14:1-3, NKJV

Secondly, the phrase *times of the Gentiles* speaks of Israel's domination by Gentile empires, such as the Roman Empire in Jesus' day. In the Seventh Chapter of Daniel, the prophet sees a vision of four great beasts that represent four great Gentile kingdoms; *the lion*, Babylon, *the bear*, Medo-Persia, *the leopard*, Greece, and *the monstrous beast with ten horns*, Rome (Dan. 7). The final Gentile kingdom to dominate Jerusalem will be the

Antichrist. In Revelation 13, the Antichrist is symbolically seen as the beast with seven heads and ten horns, who is like a *lion*, *leopard*, and *bear*, meaning that the kingdom of the Antichrist will bear similar characteristics to the historic Gentile kingdoms depicted in Daniel 7. However, the Antichrist's kingdom will be diverse and greater than his predecessors. He will also commit the abomination of desolation, when he walks into the Jewish temple and declares himself to be God and sets up his image to be worshipped in the temple (2 Thes. 2:3-4, Rev. 13:14-16).

From this brief survey of the *Mount Olivet Discourse*, we see how Jesus' prophecies serve as a template to understand end time prophecies found in the Old Testament, as well as how they align with New Testament prophecies found in the Pauline epistles and the Book of Revelation. Whereas the typical signs such as wars, famines, earthquakes, etc., have always happened, and are not within themselves indicative of the end, their increased frequency and intensity point to prophetic fulfillment. However, among all the signs Jesus gave as indicators leading up to His return, the specific sign that indicates His return is close is the *Abomination of Desolation*.

6

WHAT IS THE ABOMINATION OF DESOLATION?

During the Mount Olivet Discourse, Jesus makes refers to a historic event that also has a futuristic reference as a major end time sign called the Abomination of Desolation. In Jesus' Mount Olivet Discourse, the Abomination of Desolation is found in the following Gospel narratives.

> Therefore when you see the 'abomination of desolation,' spoken of by Daniel the prophet, standing in the holy place" (whoever reads, let him understand) Matthew 24:15, NKJV

and

> So when you see the 'abomination of desolation,' spoken of by Daniel the prophet, standing where it ought not" (let the reader understand), "then let those who are in Judea flee to the mountains. Mark 13:14, NKJV

Speaking of this abomination of desolation, Jesus is referencing Daniel's prophecy. The NIV says it this way,

> His armed forces will rise up to desecrate the temple fortress and will abolish the daily sacrifice. Then they will set up the abomination that causes desolation.
> Daniel 11:31, NIV

According to *Strong's Hebrew Dictionary*, the word *abomination* comes from the Hebrew word *shiqqûts* which means "disgusting," i.e., something that's filthy, especially an idol or some other detestable thing. The word *desolation* comes from the Hebrew word *shāmēm*, which means to be destitute, destroy to make waste. Together the words mean a desolating sacrifice.

The Lord refers us back to Daniel for two important reasons, 1) the abomination of desolation has a historic occurrence, and 2) the abomination of desolation is a major eschatological event that precedes the Day of the Lord and His second coming. Therefore, this passage has a "double reference" meaning that the historic reference has a greater fulfillment to come in the future.

Daniel 8:11 and 11:31 records the actions of Antiochus Epiphanes IV, king of Syria who in 167 B.C., desecrated the Jewish temple. This account is also recorded in the Apocrypha (books not received by Protestants as inspired, but which are historically relevant). These books are recognized by the Catholics and others and are included in the Revised Standard Version and some King James Versions). In 1 Maccabees 1:54-64, Antiochus, upset over a defeat in Egypt, returned to Jerusalem with great fury. He killed thousands of male Jews and enslaved the women. He forbid the Jews to read the Torah and did away with all Jewish holy days and feasts. Under the threat of death, he forbade all circumcisions, and most of all, he did away with the daily sacrifice and offerings. The apex of these sacrilegious actions was when he sacrificed a pig on the altar and erected a pagan idol in the most holy place of the temple. These actions were all abominations that caused desolation and the desecration of the Jewish temple.

The sacrilege committed by Antiochus resulted in the Maccabean revolt, led by Judas Maccabeus. The Jews defeated the Syrian army and took back possession of the temple. The temple then had to be cleansed and rededicated. The first rededication occurred on the 25th of *Chislev* (December), 165 B.C. The celebration lasted eight days, and was named *Hanukkah* (dedication) and for the lighting of the menorah (sacred seven-branched candlestand). The celebration is still an important Jewish holiday, and was celebrated by Jesus referred to in John 10:22, "...the feast of the dedication and it was winter."

Due to Luke's account, many scholars believe that Jesus' prediction of the abomination of desolation was actually fulfilled in 70 A.D., when the temple was destroyed by the Roman general Titus (see Luke 21:20-24). However, there is yet a future fulfillment, because Jesus characterizes those days as being unequalled in all human history, "For then there will be great tribulation, such as has not been since the beginning of the world until this time, no, nor ever shall be. And unless those days were short-ened, no flesh would be saved…" (Mt. 24:21-22, NKJV). As bad as Titus' actions were in 70 A.D., what Jesus prophesied was not fulfilled by Titus. In the Jewish Holocaust, millions more Jews were slaughtered. However, what Jesus prophesied to come will be much worse than these.

Daniel 9:27, speaking of the events that will occur during an eschatologi-cal period known as "the Seventieth Week of Daniel" (covered in the next chapter), Daniel prophesies "…at the temple he will set up an abomina-tion that causes desolation, until the end that is decreed is poured out on him" (Daniel 9:27, NIV). Also, in 2 Thes. 2:3-4, Paul gives his insight into the abomination of desolation,

> "…and the man of sin is revealed, the son of perdition, who opposes and exalts himself above all that is called God or that is worshiped, so that he sits as God in the temple of God, showing himself that he is God, 2 Thessalonians 2:3-4 (NKJV)

Paul's version of this event is interesting because the Antichrist, here called "the man of sin and the son of perdition" (or son of lawlessness), sits in the temple of God (the rebuilt Temple in Jerusalem, more on this later) and declares himself to be God. Antiochus also likened himself to God, hence the name "Epiphanes" meaning "a manifestation of God." Antiochus also took away the daily sacrifice (Dan. 11:31), and so will the Antichrist (Daniel 7:25a, 9:27).

Finally, the Antichrist, referred to as the beast in Revelation 13, like An-tiochus Epiphanes IV, he will erect an idol in the most holy place of the temple.

> And he deceives those who dwell on the earth by those signs which he was granted to do in the sight of the beast, telling those who dwell on the earth to make an image to the beast who was wounded by the sword and lived. He was granted power to give breath to the image of the beast, that the image of the beast should both speak and cause as many as would not worship the image of the beast to be killed.   Revelation 13:14-15, NKJV

Thus, Jesus spoke of this sacrilege when he prophesied, "When you see 'the abomination that causes desolation' standing where it does not belong—let the reader understand..." (Mark 13:14, NIV). It is due to these passages that point to a future fulfillment of the abomination of desolation as not only a historical event but as an eschatological one as well. This abomination of desolation will serve as one of the most defining events that signal the coming of the great tribulation, the time that has never been before, nor will ever be repeated again.

7

WHAT IS DANIEL'S SEVENTY WEEKS?

The Seventy Weeks of Daniel is where God outlines His prophetic agenda concerning the Holy City of Jerusalem, the people and nation of Israel, and is key to understanding end time prophecy. According to Daniel chapter 9:20-23, Daniel was in prayer confessing his sins and the sins of his nation Israel, who were in captivity in Babylon. For seventy long years, the Jews were in captivity in Babylon under the Chaldeans, the Medes and the Persians, as prophesied by Jeremiah in 25:11. Daniel knew the time of captivity was about to end and prayed that God would fulfill the time of their captivity (Dan. 9:3-23). Now, while Daniel was in prayer, the angel Gabriel came to give Daniel understanding concerning the "seventy weeks." Let's take a look at what the angel had to say to Daniel, beginning with verse 24:

> Seventy weeks have been decreed for your people and your holy city, to finish the transgression, to make an end of sin, to make atonement for iniquity, to bring in everlasting righteousness, to seal up vision and prophecy and to anoint the most holy place. Daniel 9:24

Since the beginning of the Jewish captivity in Babylon, Daniel lived under the rules of the Babylonian and Medo Persian empires. King Nebuchadnezzar ruled until approximately 562 B.C. His grandson, Belshazzar, took over the Babylonian throne in about 556 B.C. and ruled until he was slain in 539 B.C. Then Darius the Mede was made the ruler over the Chaldeans under the universal monarchy of Cyrus. It was Cyrus who was responsible for conjoining the forces of the Medes and the Persians. The prophet Isaiah prophesied some 150 years before Cyrus' birth that he would order the rebuilding of the temple in Jerusalem (Isa. 44:28). However, Gabriel shifts focus from the seventy years of captivity to a time period that will consist of seventy weeks of years where God will bring about His entire agenda, outlined in verse 24.

The word *week* comes from the Hebrew word *shâbûa*, which literally means "sevened," that is, "a week, specifically, of years." Just as a normal week has seven days, these weeks consist of seven years. For example, when Jacob had to serve Laban for seven years in order to marry Rachel, Genesis 29:27-28 states, "Complete *the week* of this one, and we will give you the other also for the service which you shall serve with me for another *seven years*." Jacob did so and completed her *week*...." It is clear from this text that the word "week" and seven years are used interchangeably.

Therefore, seventy weeks would equal a 490-year period (seventy weeks times seven years). Within that period, God would finish His divine agenda. However, these weeks of years have three segments; two of the segments run consecutively, while the other has a long delay before being fulfilled. Let's take a look at the passage:

> So you are to know and discern *that* from the issuing of a decree to restore and rebuild Jerusalem until Messiah the Prince *there will be* seven weeks and sixty-two weeks; it will be built again, with plaza and moat, even in times of distress. "Then after the sixty-two weeks the Messiah will be cut off and have nothing, and the people of the prince who is to come will destroy the city and the sanctuary. And its end *will come* with a flood; even to the end there will be war; desolations are determined. Daniel 9:25-26

The first segment is found in verse 25, which refers to the restoration and rebuilding of Jerusalem. Although it was Cyrus who first announced the rebuilding of the Jewish temple, it was actually King Artaxerxes who gave the permission for the city and the temple to be rebuilt in 444 B.C. (Neh. 2:1-8). In this seven-week (forty-nine years) period, this prophecy was fulfilled.

In the second segment, verse 26, we begin to count sixty-two weeks, or 434 years, from the rebuilding of the temple. However it is important to note that this prophecy of Messiah to be cut off was after the sixty-two weeks (434 years), not before or within it. Also, according to this prophetic segment, *after the sixty and two weeks* was to be the destruction of Jerusalem and the temple, which was done in 70 A.D. by Titus Flavius Vespasianus, a Roman general who would become Emperor. In Luke's account of the Mount Olivet Discourse, Jesus alludes to the destruction of Jerusalem in Luke 21:20-24. After the fulfillment of the sixty-two weeks, this brings us to a total of sixty-nine fulfilled prophetic weeks (sixty-nine times seven) totaling 483 years. Therefore, only one prophetic week is left to be fulfilled. This is the seven-year period known as Daniel's Seventieth Week.

DANIEL'S SEVENTIETH WEEK

In verse 27, we find this passage gives us a wealth of prophetic information concerning the third segment, the last remaining week.

> And he will make a firm covenant with the many for one week, but in the middle of the week he will put a stop to sacrifice and grain offering; and on the wing of abominations *will come* one who makes desolate, even until a complete destruction, one that is decreed, is poured out on the one who makes desolate. Daniel 9:27

It is during this Seventieth Week that the Antichrist, referred to as "he," will establish a *covenant with many*. This covenant will be some type of Middle Eastern peace treaty between Israel and the surrounding nations. We know this because Ezek. 38:7-10 informs us that Israel will be living safely and in peace. Additionally, 1 Thes. 5:3, states "when they say peace and safety sudden destruction shall come." Daniel 9:27 states, "And he shall confirm a covenant with many *for one week*." The covenant will be enacted for seven years. By this time Israel's temple will have been rebuilt, and animal sacrifice and the oblation (the grain offering) will have commenced under the security and backing of the Antichrist. Then three-and-one-half years later, the Antichrist will do what Antiochus Epiphanes did. He will *stop the daily sacrifice*, and place the *abomination of desolation*. In 2 Thes. 2:3-4, Paul states that he will enter the temple of God, showing himself that he is God. Then in accordance with Rev. 13:14, an image of the Antichrist will be made, and placed in the holy place of the temple, that people must worship or die.

This final week on God's prophetic calendar has been on hold since 70 A.D., when the temple was destroyed by the Romans. It is this remaining seven-year period where all of the controversy is, particularly when it comes to the rapture of the Church. This period is often referred to as the "tribulation period." In regards to the rapture of the Church (more on this later), primarily there are four main views on when the rapture will occur in relationship to the Seventieth Week. Pretribulation (pretrib), Midtribulation (midtrib), Prewrath, and Post tribulation (posttrib). All four of these theories or positions fall under the general heading of being *premillennial*. Premillennial means that these positions all believe the rapture will occur before the institution of the Lord's millennial kingdom. However, they differ as to when the rapture will occur in relationship with Daniel's Seventieth Week. *Pretrib* (the most widely held) believes the rapture will occur *before* Daniel's Seventieth Week or the tribulation comes. *Midtrib* believes the rapture will occur near the middle of the Seventieth Week. *Prewrath* believes the rapture will occur between the middle and end of the week, and *Posttrib* believes it will occur at the end of the Seventieth Week when the Lord returns.

Note: This is not an exhaustive study of all eschatological doctrines or rapture positions. Please consult with your pastor to find out which rapture position your church teaches.

8

WHO IS THE ANTICHRIST AND WHAT IS THE BEAST?

The Antichrist is the tyrannical world dictator who will rule the entire world during the last half of Daniel's Seventieth Week, a period that Jesus identified as a period of "Great Tribulation" (see Mt. 24:21). In Revelation 13, he is also called the "beast." As much as we do know about him, there is also much we do not know. It is believed he will be a man of considerable political skill in international affairs. He will be the one that Daniel 9:27 declares will confirm a covenant, or makes a strong covenant, with many (Israel and surrounding nations) for seven years. However, even though he is a political player who is involved in establishing this covenant, technically he is not the "beast" until halfway through Daniel's Seventieth Week. The Scriptures are clear: the Antichrist only has forty-two months, that is, forty-two thirty-day months, which is equivalent to three-and-one-half years (Rev. 13:5, Dan. 7:25).

Certainly, this man will be wicked. Spiritually and symbolically he is a monstrosity, but in his humanity, he will be wonderfully charismatic. The world will love him and see him as a savior. He will probably be handsome and desirable, the exact opposite of Christ, who did not have a desirable appearance (Isa. 53:2-3, NIV). Without a doubt, he will be Satan's emissary, getting his power directly from him (Rev. 13:2).

The term *Antichrist* comes from the Greek words, *anti,* which means "opposite," and *christos,* which means "Messiah" or "Christ." Together these words form the Greek word *antichristos*, which translates into the "opponent of Christ," or the Antichrist. In its singular form, the word *Antichrist* is found only four times in the New Testament, and in its plural form, it is found once. Regardless, these words are found only in the Epistles of John. For example, in 1 John 2:18, the term *Antichrist* is referring to the many who went out from them (the true believers). In this passage, those who went out denied that Jesus was the Christ, as well as His deity and equality with the Father. Since there were *"many"* (preceding) antichrists, their manifestation anticipates the coming of the epitome, the final Antichrist who is to come (1 John 2:18). The second use of the term is 1 John 2:22, "He is Antichrist, that denies the Father and the Son." John is quick to point out that a denial of Christ is a simultaneous denial of the Father, making that individual an antichrist.

The third use of the word *antichrist* in this Epistle is found in 1 John 4:3. Here, *antichrist* refers to *the lying spirits* that confess not that Jesus Christ is come in the flesh. These lying spirits probably refer to false teachers, but demonic influence cannot be ruled out. These spirits directly contradict the truth found throughout the Scriptures about the deity of Christ which says that Jesus was God manifested in the flesh (see John 1:1,14; 1 Tim. 3:16). John is countering the heretical teaching of the Gnostics who challenged the core belief that Jesus was truly human.

The final use of the term is in 2 John 7-10. In this passage, the *teachers* of the false doctrine that deny the deity of Christ, are highlighted. Of them it is said that they are deceivers; they are an antichrist.

The uses of the term in its various forms, whether it be the false teachers, individuals, or the lying spirits, are a foreshadowing of an actual person, the epitome and personification of the term. As John says, those spirits are already at work in the land and have been for a long time. It should be noted that the person, or the human ruler, who will become the Antichrist will be known to the world in two different phases, coinciding with both halves of the Seventieth Week of Daniel.

The first phase will be three-and-one-half years in length as a political statesman, whose main platform will be as a peace advocate. His second phase as an evil tyrant will also be for a three-and-one-half-year period. Technically, he's only the beast, or Antichrist, the last half of the Seventieth Week. In this latter half, the Bible uses different names for him, including the "little horn" (Dan. 7:8, 11), "the beast" (Rev. 13:1-8), the man of sin, son of perdition [lawlessness or destruction] (2 Thes. 2:3-4); all these are equivalent terms for the Antichrist.

ACTIONS OF THE ANTICHRIST

The Antichrist will walk into the reconstructed Jewish temple and, from the throne of God, declare himself as God, demanding to be worshiped as God under the penalty of death. The following passages give more information about him.

1) Receives his power from Satan (Rev. 13:2).

2) The world will worship the beast (Rev. 13:4).

3) He will speak great things and blasphemies against God (Rev. 13:5, 2 Thes. 2:4, Dan.7:8).

4) He opposes all that is called God, or that is worshipped and calls himself God (2 Thes. 2:3-4).

5) He will break the treaty with Israel and take away the right to offer sacrifices at their temple (Dan. 9:27).

6) He will kill the two witnesses (Rev. 11:7).

7) He will place the abomination of desolation (Dan. 9:27, Mt. 24:15, Rev 13:14-15).

8) He will make war with the saints (Rev. 13:7, Dan. 7:25).

9) He will cause all people of the world (whose names are not written in the Lamb's Book of Life) to receive the mark of the beast that without it no one can buy or sell (Rev. 13:16-18).

10) He will lead the world in the fight against the Lord in the battle of Armageddon (Rev 17:12-14, 19:19).

11) He will launch a preemptive attack on Babylon the Great and destroy her in one hour (Rev.17:16, Rev.18:9, 17).

12) When the Lord returns, he, along with the false prophet, will be thrown alive into the lake of fire (Rev. 19:20).

THE HIDDEN POWER BEHIND THE ANTICHRIST (the Beast)

In order to get the fullest understanding of the beast, one must realize that there are three aspects of the beast: the dictator, the kingdom, and the demonic principality from the abyss.

The human dictator will confirm the covenant in Israel, then take away the sacrifice and offering, blaspheme God, place the abomination of desolation, and make war with the saints, etc. These are the actions of the man, the one whom the world will actually see.

The kingdom of the beast is shown as having ten horns with ten crowns, depicting a ten-nation alliance that will rule the world. The kingdom or government of the beast will control world economics, issue the mark of the beast, and cause those that do not take the mark to be imprisoned and killed (Rev 13:1,16:10).

The beast that ascends from the bottomless pit (the abyss) is the final aspect of the beast. The first encounter that we have with the beast from the abyss is in Revelation 11:7, where he is identified *as the beast that ascends from the abyss*. The NIV states, "the beast that comes up from the Abyss." This first mention connects the beast and the abyss and cannot be overlooked.

The abyss (bottomless pit) is a prison for demonic principalities (see Rev. 20:1-3,7), which is where the demons who possessed the maniac of Gadara pleaded with Jesus not to send them (Luke 8:31). It is the place where fallen angels are kept in reserve until the day of judgment (Jude 6, 2 Peter 2:4). It is where Satan himself will be restrained and imprisoned for a thousand years. This is the same place that the demonic aspect of the beast comes from. It is secure, impregnable, and attended to by holy angels. The following passage is essential to understanding what is restraining the revealing of the Antichrist.

> But the angel said to me, "Why did you marvel? I will tell you the mystery of the woman and of the beast that carries her, which has the seven heads and the ten horns. The beast that you saw was, and is not, and will ascend out of the bottomless pit and go to perdition. And those who dwell on the earth will marvel, whose names are not written in the Book of Life from the foundation of the world, when they see the beast that was, and is not, and yet is." Revelation 17:7-8, NKJV

From Rev. 11:7 and 17:8, it is clear that there is a demonic aspect of the beast that comes up from the abyss. This information is critical when determining what is restraining or holding back the revealing of the Antichrist (2 Thes. 2:6-7). A greater detailed discussion on how this impacts popular rapture theories is unpacked in *Revelation Revolution, the Antichrist, Angels, and the Abyss.*

9

WHO IS THE FALSE PROPHET?

The false prophet will be a miracle-working clergyman with world-wide influence referred to in Revelation 13 as the "second beast" who works alongside the Antichrist in deceiving and controlling the world. In the Mount Olivet Discourse, Jesus declared that "false christs and false prophets will rise and show great signs and wonders to deceive, if possible, even the elect" (Mt. 24:24). Though this passage does not specifically point to the false prophet of Revelation, certainly he is within the purview of this prophecy, emphasizing the rise of false prophets during the last days. For a full examination of the subject of false prophets, please refer to *Counterfeit Charisma: The Age of False Prophets*. The following passage gives us a glimpse into the actions of this hell-inspired diabolical prognosticator.

> Then I saw another beast coming up out of the earth, and he had two horns like a lamb and spoke like a dragon. And he exercises all the authority of the first beast in his presence, and causes the earth and those who dwell in it to worship the first beast, whose deadly wound was healed. He performs great signs, so that he even makes fire come down from heaven on the earth in the sight of men. And he deceives those who dwell on the earth by those signs which he was granted to do in the sight of the beast, telling those who dwell on the earth to make an image to the beast who was wounded by the sword and lived. He was granted *power* to give breath to the image of the beast, that the image of the beast should both speak and cause as many as would not worship the image of the beast to be killed.
>
> Revelation 13:11-15, NKJV

In the above passage, he is called "another beast that rises out of the earth," and in Rev. 16:13, 19:20 he is actually called the *false prophet*. It is unknown from where this religious world leader will rise, or what religious affiliation, if any, he will spring up from. No identifying information is given about him as to his country of origin, or his ethnicity. However, what we do know is symbolically he has two horns like a lamb. This could mean in his presentation, he is not a monstrosity as the first beast that has seven heads and ten horns. No, the false prophet looks like a lamb, or is Christ-like, or a religious leader. But, though he looks like a lamb, he speaks as a dragon, which means he gives a Satanic message and is a deceiver. Paul warns, "And no wonder! For Satan himself transforms himself into an angel of light" (2 Corinthians 11:14, NKJV). The false prophet will have the same international authority as the beast. Some even believe that he could be a future Pope because of his international influence.

In many ways the false prophet is just as diabolical as the Antichrist, and arguably, even more so. Much of what is normally attributed to the Antichrist (i.e., the mark of the beast) is actually initiated by the false prophet. He will possess miracle-working power, such as calling fire down from heaven, as did the prophet Elijah (1 Kings 18:37-38, 2 Kings 1:10). It will be the false prophet who causes the world to worship the beast, and is the one who calls for an image of the beast to be made (vs.14). He then has power to *give life to the image of the beast* (vs.15). Whether this miracle falls in the same category as the magicians of Egypt whose rods became snakes (Ex. 7:11-12), or the false prophet has the power to energize this inanimate image using technology, perhaps even advanced robotics with artificial intelligence. The effect would appear to be the same.

It is understandable that a first-century writer would have no language to explain 21st century technology. There was no ancient Greek words for computer chip, microprocessor, or artificial intelligence. It is possible that to John; it appeared as though the image was actually living because John saw that the image was able to speak, and carry out an agenda to kill everyone that would not worship the beast. A lifeless robotic figure formed in the likeness of the Antichrist would indeed appear to John to be an "image." However, once turned on, it would be animated or come to life. Today, we say this about machines and technology all the time. If it's not working, we often say that it "died." If it's operational, we say it came to life.

The image of the beast could *possibly* be interfaced with data from super-computers with *artificial intelligence* and *mechanical learning* (like IBM's Watson) of the earth's populace and would determine whether someone has received the mark of the beast or not. Those who do not have the mark will not be able to buy or sell, because the image would disable their ability to participate in the economy of the beast. The image will issue the warrant to order those to be put to death. Finally, it is the false prophet, not the beast, that initiates the world receiving the mark of the beast (vs. 16-18). The false prophet and the beast will meet their fate when the Lord returns. They will be thrown alive into the lake of fire immediately without examination or trial (Rev. 19:20).

What has been put forth in the preceding paragraph are the author's thoughts on how things related to the mark of the beast and the role of the image of the beast could possibly manifest. However, scholars are not in agreement on how this and all the other events in Revelation will come to pass. It cannot be overemphasized that no one has all the answers. However, it does not mean that we have no understanding, but that no one is absolutely sure how all these things will come to pass.

10

WHAT IS THE MARK OF THE BEAST?

And he causes all, the small and the great, and the rich and the poor, and the free men and the slaves, to be given a mark on their right hand or on their forehead, and *he provides* that no one will be able to buy or to sell, except the one who has the mark, *either* the name of the beast or the number of his name. Here is wisdom. Let him who has understanding calculate the number of the beast, for the number is that of a man; and his number is six hundred and sixty-six.

Revelation 13:16-18

In 2020, every online conspiracy theorist seemed to have come out of the woodwork concerning the cause of the COVID-19 pandemic. One of these debunked theories had a piece that claimed that the mark of the beast would be given to people unawares who received the vaccine for COVID-19. This erroneous assertion once again brought the issue of the mark of the beast into the forefront. This author received several calls from concerned but uninformed Christians who had heard the mark of the beast COVID-19 vaccine conspiracy, asking could this be true? My answer was, "How can you have the mark of the beast without the beast being present?" After all, it is *his* mark. He would need to be here in his role as the Antichrist. Because of ignorance to what the Scriptures clearly teach, people have disassociated the terms Antichrist and the beast. However, these are one and the same. Therefore, the mark of the beast is impossible without the beast or the Antichrist being present and ruling.

The mark of the beast will be the way the people of the world will show their allegiance to the beast (Antichrist). This allegiance to the beast will have benefits, the first one being that you won't be incarcerated or face capital punishment for not taking the mark. Secondly, those who receive the mark will be able to participate in the economic system of the beast, who will have control over worldwide economics, banking, financial transactions of all types, whether making purchases, paying bills; all such activities will be prohibited without the mark.

Under a one-world government, economics will be controlled by an international banking system. By this point, paper money will be obsolete. European countries and much of China are already cashless. With the rise and increased usage of cash apps, even America is heading down the road to becoming a cashless society. However, under the Antichrist's regime, all jobs, occupations, associations, memberships, education, all economic transactions will be governed by the beast's worldwide economic authority.

Due to the efficiency afforded by the advanced technology, the mark of the beast will be the best economic system the world has ever known. The need for credit and debit cards that can be lost, hacked, and stolen, subject to identity theft, credit scores ruined, and many other weaknesses the current economic systems permit will be ended through having the mark of the beast. It will also eliminate black-market dealings that a cash-based society permits. Counterfeit money will also be a thing of the past.

To the world, having the mark of the beast will be the right thing to do. It will be the law. Those who refuse to get the mark will be seen as outcasts and law breakers. This will lead to people turning over violators and dissenters to the authorities. Family, friends, relatives, associates, and neighbors will turn on one another. However, in order to receive the mark of the beast, a person will have to worship the beast, which by extension means worshipping Satan. Therefore, you cannot receive the mark of the beast unaware. People will have to accept it being fully aware that they are giving their allegiance and worship to the Antichrist.

> ...And the whole earth was amazed *and followed* after the beast; **they worshiped the dragon because he gave his authority to the beast; and they worshiped the beast,** saying, "Who is like the beast, and who is able to wage war with him?" Revelation 13:3-4

And it was given to him to give breath to the image of the beast, so that the image of the beast would even speak and cause as many as do not worship the image of the beast to be killed. Rev. 13:15

And he causes all, the small and the great, and the rich and the poor, and the free men and the slaves, to be given a mark on their right hand or on their forehead, and *he provides* **that no one will be able to buy or to sell,** except the one who has the mark, *either* the name of the beast or the number of his name. Rev. 13:16-17

There have been many theories as to what the mark will be. In the past, theorists have claimed bar codes were the mark. Some say it is a computer chip that is inserted below the skin. Others have said it could be something as a QR code like the ones the people in China are issued to buy or sell goods. Some say it will be some type of tattoo. The fact is that no one knows for sure. Will there be some type of technology component to it interfaced with a globally controlled banking system? Most likely, yes. Since the world is in a state of advanced technology now, it makes sense that whatever technology is available at the time will be used by the beast.

Whatever the mark will be, it will obviously be something that promotes conformity and readily identifies the followers of the beast as being part of his kingdom. In communist and socialist societies, public conformity is a key aspect of controlling the masses. Therefore, whatever the mark is, it will be an open display, and most likely not be something one could hide, as would be the case with an implanted computer chip. It will be in the forehead or the right hand. Absolute conformity and worship will be required.

WHAT HAPPENS IF A PERSON TAKES THE MARK?

The Bible has an unambiguous warning about those who take the mark of the beast.

A third angel followed them and said in a loud voice: "If anyone worships the beast and its image and receives its mark on their forehead or on their hand, they, too, will drink the wine of God's fury, which has been poured full strength into the cup of his wrath.

They will be tormented with burning sulfur in the presence of the holy angels and of the Lamb. And the smoke of their torment will rise for ever and ever. There will be no rest day or night for those who worship the beast and its image, or for anyone who receives the mark of its name." This calls for patient endurance on the part of the people of God who keep his commands and remain faithful to Jesus. Rev. 14:9-12, NIV

Once again, this announcement precludes the fact that a person can take the mark unaware, because this warning is announced to everyone. The world will be informed that they will be tormented with burning sulfur (fire) without rest day or night, for ever and ever. More details about this eternal punishment are found in Revelation 20:14. Since the punishment is irreversible, God sends an angel to warn people not to take the mark of the beast.

However, there has been a discussion among some Evangelicals like Dr. John MacArthur, who teaches that one can still be redeemed after taking the mark. However, Dr. MacArthur and others that teach this have directly contradicted the Scriptures. His reasoning is that this is not the *unpardonable sin.*

Dr. MacArthur and others claim you can repent from any sin, therefore, so can one repent after receiving the mark of the beast. However, taking the mark of the beast is a *unique* sin that can only be committed once in human history. Only the people living at the time can commit this sin. Taking the mark of the beast can only be committed once the beast is in power. No other generation of people could have committed this particular sin, because it is attached to a particular person, the beast. Therefore, you cannot categorize this sin with others that have been committed by humanity since the beginning of time. This is a unique sin, and because of that, God gives a specific prohibition against this particular act. For the last 2,000 years now, the Book of Revelation has had this warning in it, and the warning will be given again via an angelic declaration during the time of the beast. Do not be deceived by anyone! There will be no excuse or turning back from taking the mark of the beast.

In Revelation 16, the wrath of God is poured out on the world. The first thing on his list to target are those who have taken the mark of the beast.

This is worth emphasizing. "The first angel went and poured out his bowl on the earth; and it became a loathsome and malignant sore on the people who had the mark of the beast and who worshiped his image" (Rev.16:2). Those who have the mark of the beast will be stricken with nasty, rotting, cancerous sores. Remember, the mark will be on people's foreheads, so their faces will break out with ugly, putrid sores that cannot be hidden or cured.

Finally, the most decisive argument against being saved after receiving the mark of the beast is found in the following verses. The first is Rev. 13:8 "All inhabitants of the earth will worship the beast—**all whose names have not been written in the Lamb's book of life**, the Lamb who was slain from the creation of the world." The second is Rev. 17:8, "... **The inhabitants of the earth whose names have not been written in the book of life from the creation of the world will be astonished when they see the beast....**" Both passages declare that the ones who take the mark, their names *are not* written in the Lamb's book of life. At the great white throne judgment, anyone whose name *is not* written in the book of life is thrown into the lake of fire, which is the second death (Rev. 20:14-15). This is the same punishment declared in Rev.14:9-11, for those who take the mark of the beast. It is impossible to be redeemed once you take the mark, no matter what MacArthur or anyone else says. Whether or not, a person repents, isn't the issue. The insurmountable problem is their names are not written in the Lamb's Book of Life.

This cursory review of the mark of the beast is to point out that the mark cannot occur until the beast (Antichrist) is ruling the world. Secondly, the *abomination of desolation* must be in place. Thirdly, the temple must be in place in Israel, and finally, the miracle-working false prophet who calls down fire from heaven must be ruling alongside the Antichrist. If all these things are not in place, no matter what anyone claims, it's not the mark of the beast.

As to the number 666, besides being the number of a man, no one knows exactly what this means. Perhaps as we get closer, God will impart the wisdom to decipher its meaning. However, whether someone calculates his name before he emerges or not, does not really matter. However, when it is time for him to be revealed, the world will definitely know who he is. The Antichrist will make sure of that.

11

WHAT IS ARMAGEDDON?

Armageddon is a plain in Israel where the battle of Armageddon will be fought. This battle occurs during the sixth bowl judgment of the wrath of God. "Then they gathered the kings together to the place that in Hebrew is called Armageddon" (Revelation 16:16, NIV). This is the only place in the Bible where the word *Armageddon* is found. Other translations such as the *Complete Jewish Bible* translate it as *Har Meggiddo*. In the NASB it is *Har-Magedon*. *Har* meaning "mountain," which could indicate the hilly terrain around the plain of Megiddo, some sixty miles north of Jerusalem. Since ancient history, hundreds of battles have been fought in this plain, and some are documented in the Scriptures (Judges 5:19, 2 Kings 23:29, 2 Chron. 35:22). The plain of Meggido is a natural battleground. It is reported that French statesman and military leader Napoleon Bonaparte commented that all the armies of the world could mobilize in this great plain.

During the final battle of this age, the Valley of Jezreel, where Megiddo is located, will be where the nations of the world, under demonic influence, will gather their armies to fight the returning King of Kings, Jesus Christ, the Messiah. This final conflagration will be the climactic campaign of the Day of the Lord. The following passage depicts this scene.

> Then the sixth angel poured out his bowl on the great river Euphrates, and its water was dried up, so that the way of the kings from the east might be prepared. And I saw three unclean spirits like frogs *coming* out of the mouth of the dragon, out of the mouth of the beast, and out of the mouth of the false prophet. For they are spirits of demons, performing signs, *which* go out to the kings of the earth

and of the whole world, to gather them to the battle of that great day of God Almighty. "Behold, I am coming as a thief. Blessed *is* he who watches, and keeps his garments, lest he walk naked and they see his shame." And they gathered them together to the place called in Hebrew, Armageddon. Revelation 16:12-16 (NKJV)

The battle of Armageddon will be the bloodiest battle in history, where the Lord will slay the armies of the world under the leadership of the Antichrist. Imagine a bloodbath so great that blood flows to the horses' bridles (approximately four feet deep) for 180 miles! Here is what it will be like when the Lord returns.

And I saw heaven opened, and behold, a white horse, and He who sat on it *is* called Faithful and True, and in righteousness He judges and wages war. His eyes *are* a flame of fire, and on His head *are* many diadems; and He has a name written *on Him* which no one knows except Himself. *He is* clothed with a robe dipped in blood, and His name is called The Word of God. And the armies which are in heaven, clothed in fine linen, white *and* clean, were following Him on white horses. From His mouth comes a sharp sword, so that with it He may strike down the nations, and He will rule them with a rod of iron; and He treads the wine press of the fierce wrath of God, the Almighty.

And I saw the beast and the kings of the earth and their armies assembled to make war against Him who sat on the horse and against His army. Revelation 19:11-15, 19

All the nations of the world will be involved (Zech. 14:2). However, the principals shall be the kings of the east with their 100-million-man army (Rev 9:14-16,16:12): Gog and Magog (Russia), along with Persia (Iran), Libya, Ethiopia, Turkey (Torgarmah and Gomer), and many others. Though all of these armies may come to the plain of Megiddo for differ- ent reasons, once all gathered there, they will combine their efforts and focus on the invasion from heaven.

Science fiction has always intrigued people with the idea of a hostile force invading the earth. Well, that's exactly what's going to happen in the battle of Armageddon. However, it will not be *little green men, the*

Transformers, the Klingons, or any other subterfuge Satan has sown into the heart of humanity. It will be the Lord himself on a white horse and the armies of heaven following him. The earth will be invaded by heaven's army. The world's armies gathered to fight against the Lord will be slaughtered without mercy.

The Psalmist chimes in on the folly of the nations that dare stand against God.

> Why are the nations in an uproar and the peoples devising a vain thing? The kings of the earth take their stand And the rulers take counsel together Against the LORD and against His Anointed, saying, "Let us tear their fetters apart And cast away their cords from us!" He who sits in the heavens laughs, The Lord scoffs at them. Then He will speak to them in His anger And terrify them in His fury..." Psalm 2:1-6

Isaiah also prophesies about the nations when he writes,

> Behold, the nations *are* as a drop of a bucket, and are counted as the small dust of the balance: behold, he taketh up the isles as a very little thing. And Lebanon *is* not sufficient to burn, nor the beasts thereof sufficient for a burnt offering. All nations before him *are* as nothing; and they are counted to him less than nothing, and vanity. Isaiah 40:15-17, KJV

What chance does any human or demonic kingdom have against God? Absolutely none. Yet, because they have been turned over to strong delusion (2 Thes. 2:10-12), they will be deceived by Satan through the false prophet and the Antichrist to fight in a battle they have no chance not only of winning, but of surviving.

In a final note of interest, in Ezekiel's prophecy, the Scriptures declare that the weapons will be burned.

> Then those who inhabit the cities of Israel will go out and make fires with the weapons and burn *them*, both shields and bucklers, bows and arrows, war clubs and spears, and for seven years they will make fires of them. They will not take wood from the field or gather

firewood from the forests, for they will make fires with the weapons; and they will take the spoil of those who despoiled them and seize the plunder of those who plundered them, declares the Lord GOD. Ezekiel 39:9-10

This passage has stumped scholars for years. Today, weapons are made of various types of metal alloys. So, how is it possible that they will burn the weapons? One expositor has said that this proves the weapons would be made of wood. Even though this scholar did not have in mind what I am about to suggest, he may not have been too far off.

In 2018, an article came out in *Scientific American* about a new process that makes wood harder than steel. The wooden material can be molded into any shape and can be used to replace things that steel was used for, but is cheaper and much lighter. Perhaps a technology like this one could produce low-cost, lightweight, military-grade weaponry made of wood. They are already saying that cars and planes can be made from it. They can also make it transparent.

Though it is not certain this is what the Bible speaks of, that being the case, it is possible that weapons could literally burn because one day they could make them out of wood. Again, I cannot state with certainty this is how Ezekiel's prophecy will be fulfilled. However, it does present an interesting possibility considering this new process that didn't exists until the 21st century.

12

What is the Rapture of the Church?

The rapture is when Christ miraculously takes the Church (the living saints) out of the world, being "caught up" to meet the Lord in the air prior to His outpouring of wrath on the world. The rapture comes immediately after the resurrection of the dead, because the dead in Christ shall rise first. There are a few New Testament Scriptures that directly and indirectly support the idea of the rapture. In the Gospel of John, Jesus declared,

Do not let your heart be troubled; believe in God, believe also in Me. "In My Father's house are many dwelling places; if it were not so, I would have told you; for I go to prepare a place for you. "If I go and prepare a place for you, I will come again and receive you to Myself, that where I am, *there* you may be also. John 14:1-3

In 1 Thessalonians, the apostle Paul writes,

For this we say to you by the word of the Lord, that we who are alive and remain until the coming of the Lord, will not precede those who have fallen asleep. For the Lord Himself will descend from heaven with a shout, with the voice of *the* archangel and with the trumpet of God, and the dead in Christ will rise first. Then we who are alive and remain will be caught up together with them in the clouds to meet the Lord in the air, and so we shall always be with the Lord.
1 Thessalonians 4:15-17

In 1 Corinthians, Paul also writes,

> Behold, I tell you a mystery; we will not all sleep, but we will all be changed, in a moment, in the twinkling of an eye, at the last trumpet; for the trumpet will sound, and the dead will be raised imperishable, and we will be changed. 1 Corinthians 15:51-52

However, the word *rapture* is not found in the Bible, but comes from the Latin word *rapturo*, which means to be "snatched or carried away." The word used in the Bible, which is translated as "caught up," is the Greek word *harpazo*.

Characteristics of the rapture are that it is *instantaneous*, happening in the "twinkling of an eye" (1 Cor. 15:52). The dead in Christ rise first (1 Cor. 15:52, 1 Thes. 4:16). It happens at the last trumpet (1 Cor. 15:52). Believers meet the Lord in the air (1 Thes. 4:17). No man knows the day or the hour (Mt. 24:36).

Among those in the Premillennial camp (the belief that Christ will return prior to the Millennium), much controversy exists concerning the timing of the rapture in relationship with Daniel's Seventieth Week. *Pretrib* believes the rapture will occur *before* Daniel's Seventieth Week or the tribulation comes. *Midtrib* believes the rapture will occur near the middle of the Seventieth Week. *Prewrath* believes the rapture will occur between the middle and end of the week, and *Posttrib* believes it will occur at the end of the Seventieth Week when the Lord returns.

If you are not sure where your church stands on the rapture doctrines, ask your pastor. However, the most popular and widely accepted rapture doctrine is the pretribulational rapture position. In this position, the Church gets raptured before all the trouble starts and does not go through the vast majority of the events stated in Revelation. However, there are some fundamental problems with this position that are covered in detail in this writer's end time apologetics series titled *Revelation Revolution, the Antichrist, Angels, and the Abyss*.

As it relates to the timing of the rapture, the important thing to remember about *any* of the rapture doctrines is that these are all "theories," which means they are unproven. No one has all the answers, because no one can figure how God is going to do something, even when we know what He is going to do. No matter what position you hold, when the rapture occurs, whether it's pre, mid, prewrath, or posttrib, if you are born again, you will be raptured. It doesn't matter when the Lord comes for the Church—that's not the big issue, anyway. If you die in the Lord, you'll be raised first. If you are alive when He comes, you will be caught up. Though scholars and theologians will argue their positions, the truth is the mystery of the rapture is beyond all of us. However, whether the rapture happens today or one hundred years from now, the important thing is, when the Lord comes to take the Church in the rapture, or to take you individually, will you be ready?

13

What is the Second Advent?

The Second Advent (coming) is when the Lord returns the second time to rule the earth from Jerusalem for a thousand years during the Millennium (see chapter on the Millennium). During his First Advent, Jesus came as the suffering servant, the lamb of God, to die for the sins of the world. In His Second Advent, Jesus comes back to rule as King of Kings and Lord of Lords, where He will rule the nations with a rod of iron.

There are several passages in the Old and New Testaments that speak of this event. The following are just a few passages.

And then the sign of the Son of Man will appear in the sky, and then all the tribes of the earth will mourn, and they will see the SON OF MAN COMING ON THE CLOUDS OF THE SKY with power and great glory. "and he will send forth his angels with A GREAT TRUMPET and THEY WILL GATHER TOGETHER His elect from the four winds, from one end of the sky to the other. Matthew 24:30-31

For after all it is *only* just for God to repay with affliction those who afflict you, and *to give* relief to you who are afflicted and to us as well when the Lord Jesus will be revealed from heaven with His mighty angels in flaming fire, dealing out retribution to those who do not know God and to those who do not obey the gospel of our Lord Jesus. These will pay the penalty of eternal destruction, away from the presence of the Lord and from the glory of His power, when He comes to be glorified in His saints on that day, and to be marveled at among all who have believed—for our testimony to you was believed. 2 Thessalonians 1:6-10

BEHOLD, HE IS COMING WITH THE CLOUDS, And every eye will see Him, even those who pierced Him; and all the tribes of the earth will mourn over Him. So it is to be. Amen. Revelation 1:7

And I saw heaven opened, and behold, a white horse, and He who sat on it *is* called Faithful and True, and in righteousness He judges and wages war. His eyes *are* a flame of fire, and on His head *are* many diadems; and He has a name written *on Him* which no one knows except Himself. *He is* clothed with a robe dipped in blood, and His name is called The Word of God. And the armies which are in heaven, clothed in fine linen, white *and* clean, were following Him on white horses. From His mouth comes a sharp sword, so that with it He may strike down the nations, and He will rule them with a rod of iron; and He treads the wine press of the fierce wrath of God, the Almighty. And on His robe and on His thigh He has a name written, "KING OF KINGS, AND LORD OF LORDS." Revelation 19:11-16

There are two aspects that must be distinguished: Christ coming *for His saints* at the *rapture*, and Christ coming *with His saints* at His second coming. At the rapture He meets the saints in the air. His feet do not touch the ground. In his coming *with the saints* during the culminating event of the period called the Day of the Lord, He touches down on the Mount of Olives, the same place He revealed the events to His disciples concerning the end of the age in the Mount Olivet Discourse. Zechariah gives us a glimpse of the awesome day.

Then the LORD will go forth and fight against those nations, as when He fights on a day of battle. In that day His feet will stand on the Mount of Olives, which is in front of Jerusalem on the east; and the Mount of Olives will be split in its middle from east to west by a very large valley, so that half of the mountain will move toward the north and the other half toward the south. You will flee by the valley of My mountains, for the valley of the mountains will reach to Azel; yes, you will flee just as you fled before the earthquake in the days of

Uzziah king of Judah. Then the LORD, my God, will come, and all the holy ones with Him! Zechariah 14:3-5

In pretrib, midtrib, and prewrath positions, all share the belief that the Lord coming *for* his saints and his coming *with* his saints are two different events. However, posttrib would have the two events occurring simultaneously during the second coming. Consult with your pastor to learn which position your church teaches.

14

What is the Millennium?

The word *millennium* comes from the Latin words *mille*, meaning "thousand," and *annum*, meaning "year." The Millennium is a thousand-year period during which the Lord will institute His kingdom immediately after His *Second Advent*. The primary Scripture that speaks about the thousand-year reign is found in Revelation 20.

> Then I saw thrones, and they sat on them, and judgment was given to them. And I *saw* the souls of those who had been beheaded because of their testimony of Jesus and because of the word of God, and those who had not worshiped the beast or his image, and had not received the mark on their forehead and on their hand; and they came to life and reigned with Christ for a thousand years. Revelation 20:4

From this passage we see that Christ will have a thousand-year reign with the assistance of the saints that refused to take the mark of the beast. Another important aspect of the Millennium is that Satan will be imprisoned in the Abyss during this time and will be completely inactive, being prohibited from influencing or deceiving.

> Then I saw an angel coming down from heaven, holding the key of the abyss and a great chain in his hand. And he laid hold of the dragon, the serpent of old, who is the devil and Satan, and bound him for a thousand years; and he threw him into the abyss, and shut *it* and sealed *it* over him, so that he would not deceive the nations any longer, until the thousand years were completed; after these things he must be released for a short time. Revelation 20:1-3

It is during this time that Christ will rule from Jerusalem. The nations will be required to come to worship with consequences of no rain if they do not comply.

> Then the survivors from all the nations that have attacked Jerusalem will go up year after year to worship the King, the LORD Almighty, and to celebrate the Festival of Tabernacles. If any of the peoples of the earth do not go up to Jerusalem to worship the King, the LORD Almighty, they will have no rain. If the Egyptian people do not go up and take part, they will have no rain. The LORD will bring on them the plague he inflicts on the nations that do not go up to celebrate the Festival of Tabernacles. Zechariah 14:16-18, NIV

During Christ's millennial reign, no wickedness will be allowed to prevail, as opposed to the current world that is motivated by the love of money, from which every sort of evil flows. For example, corporations that sell wicked products that cause and promote addiction, poor health, and even death will not be operating. The Lord will cause the earth to be replenished and flourish. Carnivorous animals such as lions will become herbivores, and poisonous creatures such as venomous snakes will be harmless. Another aspect of current life that will be arrested will be premature death through sickness and disease. The people will even return to *antediluvian* (before the flood) longevity. Their days shall be the days of a tree—hundreds of years. A child shall die at 100 years old!

> I will rejoice over Jerusalem and take delight in my people; the sound of weeping and of crying will be heard in it no more. "Never again will there be in it an infant who lives but a few days, or an old man who does not live out his years; the one who dies at a hundred will be thought a mere child; the one who fails to reach a hundred will be considered accursed. They will build houses and dwell in them; they will plant vineyards and eat their fruit. No longer will they build houses and others live in them, or plant and others eat. For as the days of a tree, so will be the days of my people; my chosen ones will long enjoy the work of their hands. They will not labor in vain, nor will they bear children doomed to misfortune; for they will be a people blessed by the LORD, they and their descendants with them. Before they call I will answer; while they are still speaking I will hear. The wolf and the lamb will feed together, and the lion will

eat straw like the ox, and dust will be the serpent's food. They will neither harm nor destroy on all my holy mountain," says the LORD. Isaiah 65:19-25, NIV

During this time, the Lord will make everything right. For those who have been oppressed, here's what the Lord promises, "No longer will they build houses and others live in them," and "they will not labor in vain, nor will they bear children doomed to misfortune." An important thing to remember is, the Deliverer never comes to save the oppressor, but he always comes to save the oppressed.

There are three primary millennial views: *postmillennialism, amillennialism, and premillennialism.*

Postmillennialism was once popular but today is a minority view. This position espouses that Christ would build His church over a millennium (1,000-year period), then return in his Second Advent. However, the passing of time has disproven this approach, as the Church has been on earth for 2,000 years now. The Millennium in this scheme is a silver age where there will be unprecedented advances of the Gospel throughout the world.

Amillennialism asserts that there is *no* millennium to be expected, except for that which is in progress now in this gospel age. Some in this camp believe that the saints who reign with Christ in Rev. 20:4 represent the Church age now. Some Amillennialists believe that Satan is currently bound, a position that, given all of the sin and corruption in the world, would be difficult to substantiate. This position spiritualizes the "kingdom age," where Old Testament Zion is spiritually the Church.

Premillennialism asserts that the current age will end in judgment at the second coming of Christ, who at that time will restore the kingdom to Israel and reign for at least 1,000 years. Premillennialists typically draw a tight distinction between the Church and Israel, God having separate programs for each. In the Old Testament, God's focus was on Israel. However, after Israel rejected Christ, God shifted focus to a new spiritual organism called the Church, which was a mystery hidden from the foundation of the world (Eph. 3:1-12). After the rapture of the Church, the

Lord shifts focus back to Israel and establishes His millennial kingdom with them after His Second Advent, where he reigns for a thousand years in accordance with Rev. 20:4.

Once again, no one position holds all the answers. The Millennium is yet to come, and until that time, many questions are going to go unanswered. Though there are Scriptures that speak about the Millennium, for such an expansive amount of time, there is relatively little known about it.

15

What Are the Two Resurrections?

In the following passage, Jesus speaks of two general resurrections, the *resurrection of life*, and a *resurrection of condemnation.* "Do not be amazed at this, for a time is coming when all who are in their graves will hear his voice and come out—those who have done what is good will *rise to live*, and those who have done what is evil will *rise to be condemned* (John 5:28-29, NIV). Daniel also speaks of two resurrections, "And many of those who sleep in the dust of the earth shall awake, Some to *everlasting life*, Some to *shame and everlasting contempt*" (Daniel 12:2, NKJV). In the Book of Revelation, we learn that a thousand years separate the two resurrections.

> And I saw thrones, and they sat on them, and judgment was committed to them. Then *I saw* the souls of those who had been beheaded for their witness to Jesus and for the word of God, who had not worshiped the beast or his image, and had not received *his* mark on their foreheads or on their hands. And they lived and reigned with Christ for a thousand years. **But the rest of the dead did not live again until the thousand years were finished. This is the first resurrection.** Blessed and holy is he who has part in the first resurrection. Over such the second death has no power, but they shall be priests of God and of Christ, and shall reign with Him a thousand years. Revelation 20:4-6, NKJV

In this passage, we see that those in the first resurrection are characterized as "blessed and holy." The second group, called "the rest of the dead," are not brought back to life until one thousand years after the first resurrection. Those of the first resurrection are from both Old and New Testament times. These will be the citizens of heaven and the Millennium, who will live with God for all eternity. In John, Jesus called the place that he was going to prepare for us "his father's house," the place of many mansions. There, all the redeemed will live for eternity, in heavenly bliss with God Himself, and all the heavenly host.

THE GREAT WHITE THRONE (THE Resurrection of Damnation)

> Then I saw a great white throne and Him who sat on it, from whose face the earth and the heaven fled away. And there was found no place for them. And I saw the dead, small and great, standing before God, and books were opened. And another book was opened, which is *the Book of Life*. And the dead were judged according to their works, by the things which were written in the books. The sea gave up the dead who were in it, and Death and Hades delivered up the dead who were in them. And they were judged, each one according to his works. Then Death and Hades were cast into the lake of fire. **This is the second death. And anyone not found written in the Book of Life was cast into the lake of fire.** Revelation 20:11-15, NKJV

From this passage, we learn that one thousand years after the first resurrection, the Great White Throne Judgment will occur. Characteristically, this judgment is for the unrighteous. These are judged according to their actions recorded in "the books." This is a terrifying thought that every word, thought, and deed will be judged. However, these do not have a Savior because they have rejected the Lord's saving and atoning sacrifice and did not believe the Gospel message in order to be saved. So now they must answer for themselves, before a holy and righteous God. These will be summoned up from "the sea and the dead who were in it, and Death and Hades delivered up the dead who were in them." Since these are the wicked dead, after they give account for their lives, their names are then checked against the names found in the *Lamb's Book of Life*. "And anyone not found written in the Book of Life was cast into the lake of fire," the eternal hell.

It is interesting that if you are saved, you are born physically, and then "born again." In other words, born twice, and die once. If you are not saved, you are born once (physically) but die twice. The second death occurs after being judged in the Great White Throne Judgment. Those whose names are not written in the *Lamb's Book of Life* will be thrown into the lake of fire for eternity. This is the second death.

The resurrection from the dead is a fundamental aspect of the Christian faith.

> Now if Christ is preached that He has been raised from the dead, how do some among you say that there is no resurrection of the dead? But if there is no resurrection of the dead, then Christ is not risen. And if Christ is not risen, then our preaching *is* empty and your faith *is* also empty. Yes, and we are found false witnesses of God, because we have testified of God that He raised up Christ, whom He did not raise up—if in fact the dead do not rise. For if *the* dead do not rise, then Christ is not risen. And if Christ is not risen, your faith *is* futile; you are still in your sins! Then also those who have fallen asleep in Christ have perished. If in this life only we have hope in Christ, we are of all men the most pitiable. But now Christ is risen from the dead, *and* has become the firstfruits of those who have fallen asleep. 1 Corinthians 15:12-20, NKJV

Earlier in this chapter Paul insists that if you have not believed in Christ's resurrection, "you have believed in vain."

> Now, brothers and sisters, I want to remind you of the gospel I preached to you, which you received and on which you have taken your stand. By this gospel you are saved, if you hold firmly to the word I preached to you. Otherwise, you have believed in vain. For what I received I passed on to you as of first importance: that Christ died for our sins according to the Scriptures, that he was buried, that he was raised on the third day according to the Scriptures.
> 1 Corinthians 15:1-4, NIV

In this cursory review of the two resurrections, we have only scratched the surface of this major doctrine. There are a number of interpretations that affect how the resurrection is related to the rapture. Some positions make it simultaneous, while others separate them into different events. As is typical in this book, the author is not taking a side, but presenting the concepts to the reader.

16

WHAT IS THE JUDGMENT SEAT OF CHRIST?

The judgment seat of Christ is where all the redeemed are judged for their eternal reward. In Romans we find the following,

> But why do you judge your brother? Or why do you show contempt for your brother? For we shall all stand before the judgment seat of Christ. For it is written: *"As I live, says the LORD, Every knee shall bow to Me, And every tongue shall confess to God."* So then each of us shall give account of himself to God. Romans 14:10-12, NKJV

Again, Paul comments,

> For we must all appear before the judgment seat of Christ, so that each one may be recompensed for his deeds in the body, according to what he has done, whether good or bad. 2 Corinthians 5:10

In both passages, *the judgment seat of Christ* is the operative phrase, derived from the Greek word *bema*, which, according to *Vine's Expository Dictionary*, means "a step, a place," used to denote a raised place or platform reached by steps. It was the place of assembly. The word became used for a tribune in the law courts of Greece. From this definition we can understand that the judgment seat was a place of examination as well as determination. This is where judgments are made, and outcomes given. Who will preside over such a heavenly proceeding? The Lord himself. *The New English Bible* translates it this way, "We must all have our lives laid open before the tribunal of Christ."

It is important to understand that this judgment is not to assess penalty for sin. This judgment occurs in heaven. All those here are already saved. Their sins have been atoned for through the shed blood of Christ. Therefore, the object of this judgment is to assess the gain or loss of reward. Again, the apostle Paul gives us insight into this great heavenly event.

> For no man can lay a foundation other than the one which is laid, which is Jesus Christ. Now if any man builds on the foundation with gold, silver, precious stones, wood, hay, straw, each man's work will become evident; for the day will show it because it is *to be* revealed with fire, and the fire itself will test the quality of each man's work. If any man's work which he has built on it remains, he will receive a reward. If any man's work is burned up, he will suffer loss; but he himself will be saved, yet so as through fire. 1 Corinthians 3:11-15

In this passage, Paul's revelation into that day is quite daunting. Imagine what that day will be like, where all of our works for Christ will be evaluated by fire. Works done in the flesh, out of pride, greed, self-aggrandizement, wrong motives, would fall under the combustible types, wood, hay, and straw. Those types of works would be burned up, and the person being judged would suffer the loss. In other words, they had worked in vain.

THE CROWNS

Paul spoke of this misfortune when he states, "...that I may rejoice in the day of Christ, that I have not run in vain, neither laboured in vain. Philippians 2:16 (KJV). Paul also spoke of not being disqualified.

> Do you not know that those who run in a race all run, but *only* one receives the prize? Run in such a way that you may win. Everyone who competes in the games exercises self-control in all things. They then *do it* to receive a perishable wreath, but we an imperishable. Therefore I run in such a way, as not without aim; I box in such a way, as not beating the air; but I discipline my body and make it my slave, so that, after I have preached to others, I myself will not be disqualified. 1 Corinthians 9:24-27

Here, Paul is expressing his desire that he not run long and hard, only to be disqualified at the end and lose the prize. Therefore, he encourages all to run to win.

In Revelation, Jesus admonishes the church at Philadelphia, "Behold, I come quickly: hold that fast which thou hast, that no man take thy crown" (Rev. 3:11, KJV). The crown, Greek *stephanos*, referred to as the *victors wreath*, is symbolic of heavenly reward. The term is found in the following passages, the *crown of rejoicing*, 1 Thes. 2:19, the *crown of righteousness*, 2 Tim. 4:8, the *crown of life*, James 1:12, and the *crown of glory*, 1 Peter 5:4. The crowns represent different types of rewards the believers will receive in heaven. This is why Christians are not only to believe in Christ but also to serve the Lord in this life. "Therefore, my dear brothers, be steadfast, immovable, always excelling in the Lord's work, knowing that your labor in the Lord is not in vain" (1 Corinthians 15:58, HCSB).

THE DAY OF CHRIST

Finally, the *Day of Christ* which must be distinguish from the *Day of the Lord* where the wrath of God is poured out on the world, is where glorified Christians will be rewarded. It is during the day of Christ where the *bema seat* judgment will take place. The following passages are where we learn about the day of Christ.

> ...being confident of this, that he who began a good work in you will carry it on to completion until the day of Christ Jesus Philippians 1:6

> ...as you hold firmly to the word of life. And then I will be able to boast on the day of Christ that I did not run or labor in vain. Philippians 2:16

Other passages where this information is found are, 1 Cor. 1:8 and 1 Cor. 5:5. The same concept of reward is also found in 2 Cor. 1:14 even though the wording is "day of the Lord Jesus."

17

WHY IS THE NATION OF ISRAEL KEY
TO BIBLE PROPHECY?

Israel was God's chosen people through whom he would reveal Himself as God. It was through this nation the Lord would give his word, laws, statutes, and commandments. He would make known his love, righteousness, goodness, power, judgment, and redemption to the world. But why did he choose Israel? The answer follows.

> The LORD did not set his affection on you and choose you because you were more numerous than other peoples, for you were the fewest of all peoples. But it was because the LORD loved you and kept the oath he swore to your ancestors that he brought you out with a mighty hand and redeemed you from the land of slavery, from the power of Pharaoh king of Egypt. Deut. 7:7-8, NIV

Here is what the apostle Paul said about his countrymen Israel.

> Who are Israelites, to whom belongs the adoption as sons, and the glory and the covenants and the giving of the Law and the *temple* service and the promises, whose are the fathers, and from whom is the Christ according to the flesh, who is over all, God blessed forever. Amen. Romans 9:4-5

If there is a key piece to the eschatological puzzle, without a doubt it would be the nation of Israel. In order to understand why Israel is so key to prophecy, we must go back to the promises made to Abram. Though there were many promises made, two of them follow.

The LORD had said to Abram, "Go from your country, your people and your father's household to the land I will show you. "I will make you into a great nation, and I will bless you; I will make your name great, and you will be a blessing. I will bless those who bless you, and whoever curses you I will curse; and all peoples on earth will be blessed through you." Genesis 12:1-3

This promise has seven components:

1. I will make you into a great nation

2. I will bless you

3. I will make your name great

4. You will be a blessing

5. I will bless those who bless you

6. Whoever curses you, I will curse

7. All peoples on earth will be blessed through you

In the following passage, two more Abrahamic covenantal promises are given.

As for me, behold, my covenant is with thee, and thou shalt be a father of many nations. Neither shall thy name any more be called Abram, but thy name shall be Abraham; for a father of many nations have I made thee. And I will make thee exceeding fruitful, and I will make nations of thee, and kings shall come out of thee. And I will establish my covenant between me and thee and thy seed after thee in their generations for an everlasting covenant, to be a God unto thee, and to thy seed after thee. Genesis 17:4-7, KJV

That in blessing I will bless thee, and in multiplying I will multiply thy seed as the stars of the heaven, and as the sand which *is* upon the sea shore; and thy seed shall possess the gate of his enemies; [18] And in thy seed shall all the nations of the earth be blessed; because thou hast obeyed my voice. Genesis 22:17-18, KJV

These are all great blessings that God gave to Abraham (the father of many nations). How would God make a man at one-hundred years old, and his wife Sarah ninety years old and barren, have a son? It is because of these covenantal promises. When Abraham believed God, and hoped against hope, his faith was counted as righteousness and opened the door for the miracle baby Isaac to be born. This also established the principle of justification by faith. It is by faith that all the covenantal blessings come to God's people, beginning with the nation of Israel.

So, Abraham had Isaac (Gen. 17:19, 21:5), Isaac had Jacob (Gen. 25:21-26), and Jacob's name was changed to Israel. Israel had twelve sons (Gen. 32:28), each son becoming a tribe. Therefore, there are twelve tribes of Israel (Ex. 24:4). After King Solomon died, the twelve tribes were split into the northern and southern kingdoms. The Northern Kingdom was called the *house of Israel*, and the southern kingdom (primarily Benjamin and Judah, 1 Kings 12:12-18) the kingdom of *Judah*.

After centuries of conflicts, captivity, defeat, national backsliding, and chastisement, all God's dealings with Israel and Judah are documented throughout the various books of the Old Testament. It was prophesied that the two nations (Israel and Judah) would be brought together as one nation (Ezekiel 37:15-22). In keeping with Daniel's prophecy (Dan. 9:26), in 70 A.D., the Roman general Titus destroyed the Jewish temple and Jerusalem. The Jews were scattered throughout the nations as prophesied (Deut. 28:64, Neh. 1:8). This all changed some 2,000 years later when Isaiah's prophecy about "Israel being born in a day" (Isa. 66:8) was fulfilled on May 14, 1948. Israel became a nation after almost 2,000 years of being gone from that land as a nation. Jews from around the world returned to Israel. The land that was once barren now flourishes today (Isa. 27:6, 35:1, Ezek. 38:8). This brings us to twenty-first-century Israel, and the conflicts Israel faces through the hostile nations surrounding her in the Middle East.

The conflict between the Jews and the Islamic nations surrounding them has been deadly and continuous for both sides since Israel returned to reclaim the land given to them by God through their father Abraham (Gen. 15:18-21). Ironically, both Jew and Muslim claim Abraham as their great patriarch. Muslims call him *Ibrahim*. In the Islamic faith, Ishmael was the blessed child, not Isaac. However, in the Jewish and Christian faiths, the blessing came through Isaac; Ishmael was the rejected son. In an attempt to fulfill the prophecy concerning Abraham's fatherhood, Sarah encouraged Abraham to have relations with his Egyptian slave girl Hagar, thereby having Ishmael (Gen. 16). But this was not the Lord's plan (Gen.17:15-21). The blessing was to come through a miracle child (Isaac) who serves as a type of Christ (the miracle child, the only begotten son of Abraham, who was to be sacrificed, where God provided a substitute, representing the substitutionary sacrifice of Christ (Gen. 22). Though God did bless Ishmael too, Isaac was the child the covenantal promises would pass through. However, these two bloodlines have been at odds ever since (Gal. 4:29-31).

Therefore, much end-time prophecy centers around the nation of Israel. The passage below gives us a glimpse into the tensions that we see today in the Middle East concerning Israel and her neighbors.

> The burden of the word of the LORD against Israel. Thus says the LORD, who stretches out the heavens, lays the foundation of the earth, and forms the spirit of man within him: "Behold, I will make Jerusalem a cup of drunkenness to all the surrounding peoples, when they lay siege against Judah and Jerusalem. And it shall happen in that day that I will make Jerusalem a very heavy stone for all peoples; all who would heave it away will surely be cut in pieces, though all nations of the earth are gathered against it. Zechariah 12:1-3, NKJV

Ezekiel gives us details of the alliance headed up by Gog and Magog (Russia), along with Persia (Iran), Libya, Ethiopia, Turkey, and Gomer (Southeastern Europe), and many others, that will attack Israel in the "latter years" [end times] (see Ezek. 38 & 39).

However, as prophesied to Abraham, the father of Israel, those that bless Israel will be blessed. Those that curse Israel will be cursed. Fortunately, America has always had a very good relationship with Israel, and in 1948 was the first nation to vote recognizing Israel's right to exist as a sovereign nation. Since then, the United States has sent billions of dollars in aid to help keep Israel safe and secure. However, eventually, all the nations of the earth will be gathered against Jerusalem to battle (Zech. 14), during the days just before the Lord's Second Advent. He will touch down on the Mount of Olives (Zech. 14:4-5).

It is in Israel where the seven-year covenant backed by the Antichrist, spoken of by Daniel (9:27), will be enacted. It is in Jerusalem where Israel will build their third temple. It is that same temple where the Antichrist will commit the abomination of desolation (Mt. 24:15, 2 Thes. 2:3-4). It will be in the plain of Megiddo in Israel where the Antichrist will gather the world's armies and the battle of Armageddon will be fought. When the Lord returns His feet touch down on the Mt. of Olives (Zech. 14:1-4). He will destroy the armies and nations gathered together against Jerusalem on that great day (Rev. 19:11-21). And last but certainly not least, it was the prophecy of Daniel's Seventy Weeks, where the focus of fulfilling God's prophetic agenda for this age is centered around "thy people" (the nation of Israel) and thy "holy city" (Jerusalem), Daniel 9:24, is fulfilled.

In the following passage, Jesus gave the parable of the *fig tree*.

> Now learn the parable from the fig tree: when its branch has already become tender and puts forth its leaves, you know that summer is near; so, you too, when you see all these things, recognize that He is near, *right* at the door. "Truly I say to you, this generation will not pass away until all these things take place. "Heaven and earth will pass away, but My words will not pass away. Matthew 24:32-35

Since her formation in 1948, many prophecy enthusiasts see the *fig tree* in this passage as representing modern-day Israel. This is why it's good to "pray for the peace of Jerusalem" (Ps. 122:6). Keep your eyes on Israel, because what happens there will be indicators that the coming of the Lord is getting near.

18

WILL THERE BE A TEMPLE BUILT

IN JERUSALEM?

Israel's temple has been a central aspect of the nation's identity, worship, and relationship with God. Today, those of the Jewish faith meet in *synagogues*. According to *The Holman Illustrated Bible Dictionary*, "the synagogue of the New Testament era had its roots in the time after Solomon's temple was destroyed and the people of Judah went into Babylonian exile. Local worship and instruction became necessary. Even after the Jews returned to Jerusalem and rebuilt the temple, places of local worship continued. By the first century they were called synagogues." In Israel's history the temple represents "the" place to worship God. Unlike today's churches, which number in the millions around the globe, to the Jews there was only one temple.

TEMPLE HISTORY

There were two temples in Israel's history: Solomon's, and Zerubbabel's. However, Herod's temple of Jesus' day was actually a renovation project of the second temple (Zerubbabel's) initiated during the reign of Herod the Great. These temples were located on a prominent hill north of David's capital city Jerusalem, which he conquered from the Jebusites (2 Sam. 5:6-7), known as the "temple mount." Those there is some debate as to the exact location, most accept that the temple mount is where the *Dome of the Rock*, a holy shrine for pilgrims of the Islamic faith is today. The only remaining part of Herod's temple complex is the *Wailing Wall* (the Western wall), which is a holy site for the Jews, just west of the Dome of the Rock. Both structures are in close proximity to each other.

Solomon's temple was completed around 958 B.C. (see 2 Chron. 2) and was destroyed by the Babylonians under the command of King Nebuchadnezzar around 586 B.C. (2 Kings 25:9, Jer. 52:13). The second temple (Zerubbabel's) was dedicated around 516-520 B.C., but was desecrated by Antiochus Epiphanes, king of Syria, centuries later in 167 B.C. It was rededicated by Judas Maccabeus in 164 B.C., during the Maccabean revolt (1 Macc. 4:36-51). This rededication is where the Jewish holiday *Hanukkah*, which means *dedication,* originated.

This same temple was later seized on the *Day of Atonement* by the Roman general Pompey. Herod the Great would seize the same temple in a later campaign in about 37 B.C. He then started his temple renovation project around 20 B.C. In 70 A.D., the Roman general Titus destroyed Jerusalem and the temple. Since then, the Jews have been without a temple.

The third temple is the difficult one to understand, because you have a temple that Ezekiel sees (chap. 40-48). There is also a temple of Rev. chapter 11 which clearly fits within the time frame of Daniel's Seventieth Week. Ezekiel's temple seems to be the millennial temple. However, whether the Revelation 11 temple is the same as Ezekiel's temple is hotly debated. But for the sake of this discussion, we will focus on the necessity of "a temple" to be rebuilt in Jerusalem that would accommodate the *abomination of desolation* (Dan. 9:27, 11:31, Mt. 24:15, Mark 13:14).

Clearly, there must be a literal temple to be rebuilt, because Jesus' reference to the abomination of desolation refers to the literal temple where Antiochus Epiphanes performed his desecration of Zerubbabel's temple in 167 B.C. Jesus, using that historic occurrence as a type of what the Antichrist will do during the last half of Daniel's Seventieth Week, requires an actual temple for this abomination to occur.

The Apostle Paul gives insight into this future event when he speaks of the *man of sin* (the Antichrist) "who opposes and exalts himself above every so-called god or object of worship, so that he takes his seat in the temple of God, displaying himself as being God" (2 Thessalonians 2:4).

From *this temple*, the false prophet of Revelation 13, will also perform great miracles to deceive the world (Rev. 13:11-18).

Whether the temple that the Antichrist desecrates when he commits the actions ascribed to him, in 2 Thes. 2:3-4, is the same as Ezekiel's temple is difficult to say. On one hand if it is, that temple would need to be cleansed and rededicated. If it is the same temple, given the dimensions that Ezekiel's temple calls for, it seems doubtful, as some propose, that this could be built in three-and-one-half years, during the first half of Daniel's Seventieth Week. This would be a huge undertaking, as the Jews would take painstaking efforts and meticulous detail to construct this entire complex. This would seem to be a project that those overseeing construction would be reluctant to rush. And to avoid defiling elements of the temple, not just anyone would be allowed to work on such a holy site. Still others insist this temple could be built quickly.

Another option could be that the temple which the Antichrist desecrates will be a smaller portion of a larger project completed during the Millennium—no one knows for sure. Though many believe that the temple will be built during the first half of Daniel's Seventieth Week, there is no reason to impose that theory on a three-and-one-half-year time frame. The temple that the Antichrist desecrates could already be in place by the time the Antichrist enacts the seven-year covenant. In order to make that time framework, the temple would need to be completed and operational before the halfway point. It is at the middle of the Seventieth Week that the sacrifice and daily offering is taken away, which demands that the sacrificial services already be in place.

However, according to some Jewish scholars and rabbis, in order for Israel to build a temple, either the Messiah would have to return, or a prophet arise to hear from God to give directions on the exact site where the temple construction could begin. Other scholars say that the rebuilding of the temple does not depend on a coming Messiah. In any case, it should also be noted that there is currently *The Temple Institute* in Jerusalem, which is a museum as well as an official organization that is currently preparing the temple utensils, the priestly garments, and training for the priesthood and other functions in support of a new temple. They even have a virtual tour of the new temple that can be viewed on their website. The Temple

Institute's purposes stated on their website are, *"The range of the Institute's involvement with this concept includes education, research, activism, and actual preparation."* Clearly, any announcement by the Israeli government concerning the construction of a new temple would have tremendous end-time prophetic significance.

19

WHO ARE THE TWO WITNESSES?

Two of the most enigmatic figures of the Bible are the two witnesses of Revelation 11. The following passage gives us a glimpse of these mysterious prophets.

> And I will grant *authority* to my two witnesses, and they will prophesy for twelve hundred and sixty days, clothed in sackcloth." These are the two olive trees and the two lampstands that stand before the Lord of the earth. And if anyone wants to harm them, fire flows out of their mouth and devours their enemies; so if anyone wants to harm them, he must be killed in this way. These have the power to shut up the sky, so that rain will not fall during the days of their prophesying; and they have power over the waters to turn them into blood, and to strike the earth with every plague, as often as they desire. Revelation 11:3-6

These two prophets are probably the same individuals mentioned in the Book of Zechariah 4:3,11-14. They have 1,260 days (three-and-a-half years) to prophesy. Much controversy has been generated over who these individuals are. Though there is a popular theory, it cannot be stated with any certainty who these two individuals will be. Many claim that it will be Elijah and Moses, because these were the same two in the transfiguration (Mt. 17:1-3). Secondly, Malachi prophesied that before the Day of the Lord comes that God would send Elijah (Mal. 4:5), whereas John the Baptist came "in the spirit of Elijah" (Luke 1:17). Thirdly, just as did Elijah, these two prophets will shut up heaven so that it does not rain (1 Kings 17:1), and turn water into blood as did Moses (Ex. 7:19-20). Some go as far as to claim that since Enoch and Elijah didn't die, but was taken by God and taken into heaven via chariot of fire (Gen. 5:4, 2 Kings 2:11), in order to fulfill "...it is appointed unto men once to die, but after this the judgment" (Hebrews 9:27, KJV), he is brought back to fulfill death's appointment. Again, these are all speculations.

Once the two witnesses finish their 1,260 days of prophesying, things get interesting.

> When they finish their testimony, the beast that ascends out of the bottomless pit will make war against them, overcome them, and kill them. And their dead bodies *will lie* in the street of the great city which spiritually is called Sodom and Egypt, where also our Lord was crucified. Then *those* from the peoples, tribes, tongues, and nations will see their dead bodies three-and-a-half days, and not allow their dead bodies to be put into graves. And those who dwell on the earth will rejoice over them, make merry, and send gifts to one another, because these two prophets tormented those who dwell on the earth. Revelation 11:7-10, NKJV

As the above passage declares, once the two witnesses complete their 1,260-day time frame, they are killed by *the beast that ascends out of the bottomless pit*. This demonic principality is the actual power-player behind his human counterpart the beast (Antichrist). Once he is released from the bottomless pit (abyss), he will kill the two witnesses. Their dead bodies will lie in the streets of Jerusalem (where also our Lord was crucified), and *the whole world will see them*. This prophecy could not have been fulfilled in any other century until the twentieth and twenty-first centuries, where satellite communication and the internet would allow for news to be beamed around the planet, allowing everyone on earth to see the same event in real time.

After their deaths, there will be a three-day worldwide celebration. People will send gifts to one another, as they rejoice over these two witnesses being killed. This event will catapult the Antichrist into worldwide prominence, because no one will have been able to kill these two witnesses. As their three-and-a-half years is completed, the Antichrist's three-and-a-half years begins. Therefore, these two witnesses could not be in the second half of Daniel's Seventieth Week, but in the first half.

If one places these prophets in the second half of the 70th week, for the following reasons, that the timing does not work. (1) once they finish their three-and-a-half years, that places their death at the very end of the Seventieth Week, which means the Lord is returning at this time, after the onslaught of the divine bowl judgments of Rev. 16. The worst bowls being the sixth bowl, which starts the battle of Armageddon, and the seventh bowl, which unleashes a worldwide earthquake that is the worst since people have been on earth. All the cities of the nations fell, islands and mountains were not found. On top of that, 100-pound hail will demolish what's left. Then the Lord returns and destroys the armies gathered to oppose Him in the culmination of Armageddon.

It is quite improbable that there would be a worldwide party celebrating the death of the two witnesses occurring at the same time these last bowl judgments are striking. People will not be sending gifts to one another at the same time the Lord is returning at the end of Daniel's Seventieth Week. Also, as soon as the Lord returns, the Antichrist and the false prophet are captured and immediately thrown alive into the lake of fire (Rev. 19:20).

The final point is in reference to the two witnesses being raised from the dead.

> Now after the three-and-a-half days the breath of life from God entered them, and they stood on their feet, and great fear fell on those who saw them. And they heard a loud voice from heaven saying to them, "Come up here." And they ascended to heaven in a cloud, and their enemies saw them. Revelation 11:11-12, NKJV

Without a doubt, the two witnesses are raised from the dead three days after their three-and-a-half years is finished. That means that if they were in the second half of Daniel's Seventieth Week, they are raised from the dead after the Lord has already returned. They would be in complete conflict with the Lord returning, where every eye shall see him (Mt. 24:29-30, Rev. 1:7). Finally, this puts their resurrection three days into the Millennium, and places the worldwide celebration three days into the Millennium as well.

The next part of the account follows.

And they heard a loud voice from heaven saying to them, "Come up here." And they ascended to heaven in a cloud, and their enemies saw them. In the same hour there was a great earthquake, and a tenth of the city fell. In the earthquake seven thousand people were killed, and the rest were afraid and gave glory to the God of heaven. Revelation 11:12-13, NKJV

These final events make the second-half timing of the two witnesses untenable, because after they are raised from the dead, there is an earthquake in Jerusalem which would have to occur three days into the Millennium, after the Lord is already starting his Millennial reign. Lastly, the following passage states, "The second woe is past. Behold, the third woe is coming quickly" (vs. 14). This forces the third woe to be fulfilled in the Millennium after the Lord has already returned and the Seventieth Week is completed, which presents a fatal error for the last-half two witnesses theory.

Finally, here is how the story of the two witnesses ends.

Now after the three-and-a-half days the breath of life from God entered them, and they stood on their feet, and great fear fell on those who saw them. And they heard a loud voice from heaven saying to them, "Come up here." And they ascended to heaven in a cloud, and their enemies saw them. Revelation 11:11-12, NKJV

After being dead for three days, while the world is still celebrating their deaths, all of a sudden they come back to life and stand on their feet. Then God calls them to "come up here." While people are watching in astonishment, they lift up from the earth into heaven, which today we call the sky, or space. It is *this author's opinion* that the Antichrist will lie and claim that these must have been some type of extraterrestrial beings. How else will he explain these men coming back to life and leaving the earth in a cloud? Do you think the Antichrist will declare to the world, "read all about the two witnesses in Revelation 11?" The world will be watching in real time when these prophets "lift up" from earth in a cloud. Trust me, the Antichrist will not be giving the glory to God, but he will promote a lie that the world will believe.

The world being attacked by an invading force has been a prominent sci-fi theme since Orson Welles' broadcast, later made into a blockbuster movie titled *The War of the Worlds*. Since then, the world has been inundated with films and TV miniseries depicting the earth being invaded by aliens. In the blockbuster film *Independence Day*, the alien craft arrived shrouded in a cloud. I point out this similarity because it is a common depiction of alien forces arriving in clouds.

Now, of course, this is all science fiction and mere entertainment. And it is not the author's intention to interpret eschatology by sci-fi films, but we must understand the power of suggestion that films and television have on people's behavior and belief systems. I believe Satan has hijacked these biblical themes to propagate a mass deception by mixing lies with the truth. Revelation 1:7 reads, "Look, he is coming with the clouds," and "every eye will see him, even those who pierced him"; and all peoples on earth "will mourn because of him." So shall it be! Amen (also see Dan. 7:13). Who the world should be expecting is not an alien army, but the Lord's army.

20

WHO ARE THE 144,000?

There has been much controversy surrounding the identity of all the nation of Israel. However, we do know that even though Israel rejected Christ, and has been under *national blindness*, and cannot see Jesus as being the Messiah, there will be a point in their future where they will come to Christ. In Romans, Paul speaks of Israel's blindness when he states,

> For I do not want you, brethren, to be uninformed of this mystery— so that you will not be wise in your own estimation—that a partial hardening has happened to Israel until the fullness of the Gentiles has come in; and so all Israel will be saved; just as it is written, "THE DELIVERER WILL COME FROM ZION, HE WILL REMOVE UNGODLINESS FROM JACOB." "THIS IS MY COVENANT WITH THEM, WHEN I TAKE AWAY THEIR SINS." From the standpoint of the gospel they are enemies for your sake, but from the standpoint of *God's* choice they are beloved for the sake of the fathers.   Romans 11:25-28

The *mystery* (God's hidden truth made known to humans through revelation) of Israel's blindness became the gateway in which God opened the door to the Gentiles (Rom. 11:11). God has never totally abandoned Israel. Therefore, it should be no surprise that Israel plays a major role in end-time prophecy. Their blindness was said to be *in part* meaning that it was "temporary" while God completes His divine plan for the Gentiles (those not of the nation of Israel). Ironically, the Jews were the first Christians (see Acts 2). However, as a nation they were vehemently opposed to Christ. Spiritually, in the body of Christ, there is no "Jew or Gentile" designation as such; all are one in Christ (Rom. 10:12, Gal. 3:28, Col.3:11). However, this does not mean that Jews who accept Jesus should no longer be seen as Jews, but are in fact Jewish Christians. People do not loose their ethnicity when they become Christians. Jews are still Jews just as Greeks are still Greeks.

In 70 A.D., after Jerusalem and the temple were destroyed, Israel had not been back in that land as a nation until May 14, 1948. Jews then came back to the Holy Land, but their specific tribal identifications are not always clear. Today, many think of the nation of Israel as just being Jews. However, Jews only made up the southern kingdom, that being mainly the tribes of Benjamin and Judah. It is from the tribe of Judah where the term Jew derived. Jesus, being from the tribe of Judah, spoke of the *lost sheep of the House of Israel*, meaning the other tribes.

Since their dispersion in 70 A.D., there are different groups of Jews scattered around the world. The *Ashkenazi* Jews are from Europe. The *Maghrebi* Jews are from North Africa. The *Mizrahi* Jews include North Africa, West Asian, such as Babylonian, Kurdish, Persian, Palestinian, Egyptian, Sudanese, and Syrian Jews. *Falashim* or *Beta Israel*, also known as the Ethiopian Jews, were airlifted to Israel during *Operation Solomon* in 1991. There are also the *Kaifeng Jews, from* China. All these are just a few of all the groups of Jews/Israel that are known after being dispersed around the world during various times in the nation of Israel's history. What this means is Israel's composition is multiracial: white, black, brown, and yellow. You cannot identify Israel by looking at outward characteristics such as race alone.

However, in an eschatological sense, specific tribes are identified in Revelation 7. The passage is as follows.

> And I heard the number of those who were sealed, one hundred and forty-four thousand sealed from every tribe of the sons of Israel: from the tribe of **Judah,** twelve thousand *were* sealed, from the tribe of **Reuben** twelve thousand, from the tribe of **Gad** twelve thousand, from the tribe of **Asher** twelve thousand, from the tribe of **Naphtali** twelve thousand, from the tribe of **Manasseh** twelve thousand, from the tribe of **Simeon** twelve thousand, from the tribe of **Levi** twelve thousand, from the tribe of **Issachar** twelve thousand, from the tribe of **Zebulun** twelve thousand, from the tribe of **Joseph** twelve thousand, from the tribe of **Benjamin,** twelve thousand *were* sealed. Revelation 7:4-12

Comparing this list to 1 Chronicles 2:1-2, the sons of Israel, each representing a tribe, were Reuben, Simeon, Levi, Judah, Issachar, Zebulun, Dan, Joseph, Benjamin, Naphtali, Gad, and Asher. However, in Revelation, Manasseh is a tribe that replaces Dan.

The discussion prior to this was necessary in bringing out the point that according to Revelation 7, these tribes still exist in the earth realm. It is quite possible that there are members of these tribes who may not be aware that they are among the tribes of Israel or to which tribe they belong. Though the world may not know, God certainly does. When speaking of the blessing that Israel will enjoy during the Millennial kingdom, Isaiah gives us an interesting perspective.

> No longer will they build houses and others live in them, or plant and others eat. For as the days of a tree, so will be the days of my people; my chosen ones will long enjoy the work of their hands. They will not labor in vain, nor will they bear children doomed to misfortune; for they will be a people blessed by the LORD, they and their descendants with them. Before they call I will answer; while they are still speaking I will hear. Isaiah 65:22-24, NIV

This verse gives us a glimpse into some of the socioeconomic conditions of at least some of Israel, just prior to the Lord instituting His earthly kingdom. Isaiah declares, "No longer will they build houses and others live in them, or plant and others eat... they will not labor in vain." This implies that God will relieve them of a status of servitude, of a people who typically do not partake in the benefit of their labor because they are treated as second-class. Another important clue is "...nor will they bear children doomed to misfortune." These people bear children who typically do not have the same opportunities as others and experience the misfortunes of poverty, underemployment, poor education, and are subject to crime, danger, imprisonment, and premature death, all the manifestations of being *doomed to misfortune*. Without making a pronouncement of any type, look around. Who fits this profile? Is it the nation of Israel of the twenty-first century? Is it the European or American Jews that live like this? Where are these Israelites living under these conditions? Maybe this group, wherever they may be, do not know they are part of Israel. If we accept the premise that we are in the last days, that means this group is here now. When 12,000 members of each tribe are sealed, undoubtedly, there are going to be some surprises.

Other than the fact that these men are from the twelve tribes, little as actually known about these 144,000. Revelation 14:4-5 informs us about their holiness and character.

> These are those who did not defile themselves with women, for they remained virgins. They follow the Lamb wherever he goes. They were purchased from among mankind and offered as firstfruits to God and the Lamb. No lie was found in their mouths; they are blameless. Revelation 14:4-5, NIV

Though many insist they will be *Jewish evangelists* who preach to the world after the Church is raptured, though that cannot be ruled out, it is important to understand that assertion is not explicit in the Scriptures. Dispensationalist typically promote that narrative, but they do so without any Biblical proof. There is nothing in Scriptures whatsoever about these Israelites preaching and leading people to Christ during the tribulation. The word *evangelist* is not attached to any mention of them in the Scriptures.

Pretrib proponents claim that the great multitude seen after the 144,000 (Rev. 7:9) are supposed to come to Christ because of the soul-winning efforts of the 144,000. However, that too, is conjecture, because the Scriptures say nothing of an innumerable multitude coming to Christ through the efforts of the 144,000. Is it possible that God could use them in this way, of course. The point is, the Scriptures do not state this, scholars do.

What they will do, how they will do it, and where they will do it, and what specific role they will play is unknown. However, what we do know is that they will be chaste, holy, be sealed in their foreheads, and from the twelve tribes of Israel. In Revelation 14, they are seen on Mount Zion (during the Millennium or possibly heaven) with the Lord. They have the Lamb's and his Father's name written on their foreheads. They sang songs, were referred to as being redeemed from the earth, blameless, and were firstfruits unto God, and followed the Lamb wherever he goes. Except for what is explicitly stated about them in Scripture is mere speculation.

21

ISRAEL THE LAND OF UNWALLED VILLAGES

On May 14, 1948, Israel was reborn as a nation. However, her safety and existence have been under siege ever since. A series of wars stemming from Israel's hostile neighbors launching coordinated attacks against the Jewish state have been a persisting reality. Though there have been numerous wars and countless attacks against the small nation, Israel has valiantly repelled each one of them, and even extended her borders in the process. Israel has been involved in several wars and conflicts, however, there have been four major ones.

The War of Israel's Independence (1947-1949), against Lebanon, Syria, Iraq, Transjordan (Jordon), Egypt, Sudan, the Palestinians, and some volunteers from Arab nations. Against overwhelming odds, Israel outnumbered and outgunned its enemies, and won a stunning victory.

The Sinai Campaign (operation Kadish, 1956) was fought to put an end to the terrorist incursions into Israel and to remove the Egyptian blockade of Eilat.

The Six Day War (1967), within the brief span of six days, the Israeli Defensive Forces (IDF) on the Sinai Peninsula captured the West Bank of the River Jordan as well as, the majority of the Golan Heights. The crowning event of this amazing campaign was the capture of the Old City of Jerusalem. The historic battle cry of the IDF soldiers echoed throughout the region and around the world was, "the temple mount is in our hands."

The Yom Kippur War began on Israel's holiest holiday, *The Day of Atonement*, when Egypt and Syria launched a surprise attack, catching Israel completely off guard. This battle was the deadliest conflict since the 1948 *War of Independence*. Though Syria and Egypt made significant gains in the initial attack, within days, Israel quickly turned the tide when their army moved within artillery range of the airfields of Syria, close to the capital city of Damascus, and within 100 kilometers of Egypt's capital, Cairo, forcing Syria and Egypt to cease hostilities.

Since Israel has been back in the land, a couple of peace treaties have been attempted. The first one was the Camp David Accord, between Israel and Egypt (September 1978), signed at the Camp David retreat in Maryland, between Israeli Prime Minister Menachem Begin, Egyptian President Anwar Sadat, and United States President Jimmy Carter. Then in 1994, in another peace deal, Jordan's King Hussein and Israeli Prime Minister Yitzhak Rabin signed the Washington Accord, with United States President Bill Clinton.

Most recently, there have been three treaties that the Trump administration has brokered concerning Israel: the Arab Emirates, (August 2020) with Bahrain (September 2020) and Sudan (October 2020). Though the majority of these peace deals have, over time, fallen short, America has been at the forefront of attempting to initiate a lasting peace agreement in the region. Israel and her neighbors, all Islamic, have found it very difficult to coexist in the land. A particular trouble spot of the unsettled and ongoing conflict is with the Palestinians who were displaced when Israel returned and annexed portions of land previously occupied by the Palestinians.

All of these political issues and conflicts set the stage for what will eventually lead to the seven-year "covenant with many" backed and guaranteed by the Antichrist spoken of in Daniel 9:27. This peace treaty will start the clock to the final seven years of this age, culminating with the battle of Armageddon. It is believed by many that after this agreement is signed, Israel will finally experience a short-lived peace. However, Russia (Gog and Magog) with a coalition of Iran, Libya, Ethiopia, Turkey, and Eastern European countries will launch an attack on Israel. This ill-fated military campaign is prophesied in Ezekiel 38 and 39. However, what is key to this study is the mindset of this coalition when they say in their heart,

You will say, 'I will go up against a land of unwalled villages; I will go to a peaceful people, who dwell safely, all of them dwelling without walls, and having neither bars nor gates'... "Therefore, son of man, prophesy and say to Gog, 'Thus says the Lord GOD: "On that day when My people Israel dwell safely, will you not know *it?*

Ezek. 38:11, 14, NKJV

The Walls Are Up

This passage gives us an interesting detail: Israel will become the land of "unwalled villages." Over the years, due to all of the conflicts in the region, since 2002, Israel has erected a series of walls and fences to block hostile incursions and illegal immigration into their territory. To date Israel has hundreds of miles of walls, which have become a notable feature of its border region landscape. This is a testament to the accuracy of Scripture in prophecies written by Ezekiel over 2,500 years ago. Now Israel's walls are in place. But there will come a time after the peace deal where Israel will finally relax and take down their walls. And just as prophesied, Israel will become the *land of unwalled villages* (settlements).

During the Armageddon conflict, Zechariah gives us some important information about what will happen in Israel to Jerusalem.

Behold, the day of the LORD is coming, And your spoil will be divided in your midst. For I will gather all the nations to battle against Jerusalem; The city shall be taken, The houses rifled, And the women ravished. Half of the city shall go into captivity, But the remnant of the people shall not be cut off from the city. Then the LORD will go forth And fight against those nations, As He fights in the day of battle. And in that day His feet will stand on the Mount of Olives, Which faces Jerusalem on the east. And the Mount of Olives shall be split in two, From east to west, *Making* a very large valley; Half of the mountain shall move toward the north And half of it toward the south. Then you shall flee *through* My mountain valley, For the mountain valley shall reach to Azal. Yes, you shall flee As you fled from the earthquake In the days of Uzziah king of Judah. Thus the LORD my God will come, *And* all the saints with You.

Zechariah 14:1-5, NKJV

In this amazing passage, Israel is going to go back into captivity as the Antichrist reneges on any promises made to Israel when he breaks "the covenant with many" (Dan. 9:27). In response to Israel's perilous predicament, the Lord will return in power and glory. He will touch down on the Mount of Olives. This is interesting, because it was the Mount of Olives that Jesus disclosed to His disciples what would be the signs of his return. And it was from this same mount that Jesus was taken up into heaven (Mt. 24, Acts 1:11).

According to this passage, the mountain will split in half, creating "a very large valley." The remnant of Israel will flee into the valley that is created, where they will be protected from the divine onslaught that will occur. When the Lord returns, he won't come back alone, because the passage declares, "Thus the LORD my God will come, *And* all the saints with You. Revelation gives us the outcome of the Lord's return in regard to the beast and the world's armies gathered for the Armageddon conflict.

And I saw the beast, the kings of the earth, and their armies, gathered together to make war against Him who sat on the horse and against His army. Then the beast was captured, and with him the false prophet who worked signs in his presence, by which he deceived those who received the mark of the beast and those who worshiped his image. These two were cast alive into the lake of fire burning with brimstone. And the rest were killed with the sword which proceeded from the mouth of Him who sat on the horse. And all the birds were filled with their flesh. Revelation 19:19-21, NKJV

Revelation 14 gives a different angle on this great battle.

So the angel thrust his sickle into the earth and gathered the vine of the earth, and threw *it* into the great winepress of the wrath of God. And the winepress was trampled outside the city, and blood came out of the winepress, up to the horses' bridles, for one thousand six hundred furlongs. Revelation 14:19-20, NKJV

The carnage after this battle is beyond comprehension. The blood will flow approximately four feet deep up to a horse's bridle (bit), for approximately 200 miles. The slaughter will be so great that the Lord will call for the birds to come devour the dead carcasses (Rev. 19:17-18, Luke 17:37).

Additionally, Zechariah gives us a different angle as well when he prophesies about the plague that the Lord will strike the nations with that come against Jerusalem,

> And this shall be the plague with which the LORD will strike all the people who fought against Jerusalem: Their flesh shall dissolve while they stand on their feet, Their eyes shall dissolve in their sockets, And their tongues shall dissolve in their mouths. It shall come to pass in that day *That* a great panic from the LORD will be among them. Everyone will seize the hand of his neighbor, And raise his hand against his neighbor's hand. Zechariah 14:12-13, NKJV

When all hope seems to be lost for Israel during those final days, the Lord will return in glory and fight for His people. God will call in remembrance all those who helped and those who opposed this chosen people. Therefore, as the Psalmist implores, "Pray for the peace of Jerusalem: they shall prosper that love thee" Psalms 122:6, KJV.

22

WHAT ROLE DO ANGELS PLAY
IN END TIME PROPHECY?

A full study of angels is beyond the scope of this chapter. The following is just a cursory review of *angelology*, the study of angels. Angels play a key role in the execution of God's divine plan in the heavenlies and on earth. In the Old Testament, the Hebrew word for angel is *mal'ak*, and in the New Testament the Greek word is *angelos*. Both words mean *messenger*. Angels fall into two camps, holy and fallen. It is widely accepted that fallen angels are also equated to demons, though some distinguish between the two (Rev. 12:7-9). The term *angel of the Lord* in many cases is the Lord in angelic form (Zech. 3:1-7). There are different types of angels, such as the *seraphim* and *cherubim* (Isa. 6:2-4, Ezek.10:8-14). These are the only angelic beings said to have wings. There are *archangels*, which are high-ranking i.e., Michael (Dan. 10:13, Jude 9).

Angels carry messages from heaven to people (Gen. 16:7, Luke 1:30, Mt. 1:20). They act as mediators (Gal. 3:19). They are extremely numerous, and worship God around His throne (Rev. 5:11, Heb. 12:22). Angels can appear as humans (Heb. 13:2), or so frightening that it produces fear and trauma (Dan. 10:5-19). They are capable of immense destructive power (Gen. 19:1, 9-11,13; 2 Kings 19:35). They have power over atmospheric conditions (Rev. 7:1, Rev. 16:8) and the animals (Rev. 19:17-18). They bring judgment on humans and fallen angels, i.e., *celestial beings* (Acts 12:23, 2 Peter 2:10b-11). They minister to, protect and strengthen God's people (Ps. 34:7, Mt. 18:10, Luke 22:43, Acts 27:23, Heb. 1:14), but they are not to be worshiped (Col. 2:18, Rev. 22:9).

ANGELS IN THE LAST DAYS

Angels are prominent in the Book of Revelation and other eschatological passages in Old and New Testaments. In Daniel, the guardian of the nation of Israel, the archangel Michael, defends Israel (Dan. 12:1). In Revelation, angels are assigned to each of the seven churches of Asia Minor, though many interpret angel here to mean the pastors. Though that could be, in the text the word is "angel." Angels blow the seven trumpets unleashing judgments on the earth (see Rev. 8-9). They also pour out the bowls of wrath on the earth (Rev. 16). They are also responsible for the reaping of the wicked to be placed in the winepress of the wrath of God (Rev. 14:17-20). They unveil mysteries and truth (Rev. 10, 17). These are just a few of the actions belonging to angels in Revelation.

Angels are also the restrainers of the demonic principalities who are incarcerated in the Abyss or bottomless pit (Rev. 20:1-3). Angels are also warriors. Michael and his angels kick the devil and his angels out of heaven (Rev. 12:7-9). Satan (the chief fallen angel) is then locked in the Abyss for 1,000 years, then let loose for a while to deceive the world for the last time, and then thrown into the lake of fire forever (Rev. 20:1-3, 7-10).

Angels are present during the rapture (1 Thes.4:16) and during the second coming of Christ (Mt. 24:31, 2 Thes. 1:7). In the Scriptures, we are only given a few angelic names such as, Michael, Gabriel, Satan, and Abaddon (a fallen angel of the Abyss). In Judges 13:17-18, the angel would not tell Manoah his name. He replied, "Why do you ask my name? It is beyond understanding" (NIV). The KJV translates it, Why askest thou thus after my name, seeing it *is* secret? The NASB and others translate it "wonderful," implying *incomprehensible*. However, in both Old and New Testaments, angels are always referred to in the *masculine* gender as he, him, his, or man.

Some fallen angels are reserved in chains of darkness until the day of judgment (2 Pet. 2:4), while others are active in the earth and heavenly realms (Eph. 6:12). However, they all will face judgment and be punished eternally in the lake of fire (Rev. 20:20). Hell was made for the devil and his angels (Mt. 25:41). The final judgment and eternal damnation of all fallen angels is certain.

23

The New Heaven and Earth

After all the apocalyptic events found in the Book of Revelation, chapters 21 and 22 represent a great transition from the great tribulation to the new heaven and new earth. This comes as welcome news, where God will settle all accounts, right every wrong, and once and for all do away with all the iniquity and its effects that have plagued the human race since the fall of Adam. In the following passage, we get a glimpse of how glorious it will be in eternity with a loving, all-powerful God. As the contemporary Gospel song says, "I can only imagine...."

> Then I saw a new heaven and a new earth; for the first heaven and the first earth passed away, and there is no longer *any* sea. And I saw the holy city, new Jerusalem, coming down out of heaven from God, made ready as a bride adorned for her husband. And I heard a loud voice from the throne, saying, "Behold, the tabernacle of God is among men, and He will dwell among them, and they shall be His people, and God Himself will be among them, and He will wipe away every tear from their eyes; and there will no longer be *any* death; there will no longer be *any* mourning, or crying, or pain; the first things have passed away." And He who sits on the throne said, "Behold, I am making all things new." And He said, "Write, for these words are faithful and true." Revelation 21:1-5

There are many aspects of the new heaven and new earth that go far beyond the scope of this chapter. In your own time, please read chapters 21 and 22. It may not be a bad idea to begin a study of Revelation with these two chapters, because it reinforces the fact that no matter what happens in the tribulation, that God is always in control. In the final analysis God will turn all sorrow and pain into the blessedness and joy of the eternal state wherein righteousness dwells. Let's examine each element of the above passage.

A new heaven and a new earth; for the first heaven and the first earth passed away.

As amazing as our planet and the universe are, they have all been under a curse and subject to vanity or decay. Nothing is as it should be or functions as it should have before sin entered this reality. Because of this, all things in the entire universe are subject to atrophy. In Romans 8, Paul says it this way, "…the creation itself will also be set free from the bondage of corruption into the glorious freedom of God's children. For we know that the whole creation has been groaning together with labor pains until now" (Romans 8:21-22, HCSB).

The word *corruption* comes from the Greek word *phthora*, which means *the breakdown of organic matter, dissolution, deterioration, corruption.* This concept is explicitly stated in 2 Peter 3:10, "But the Day of the Lord will come like a thief; on that day the heavens will pass away with a loud noise, the elements will burn and be dissolved, and the earth and the works on it will be disclosed" (2 Peter 3:10, HCSB).

These texts inform us that God will literally reorder, recreate the entire creation, which since Adam has been waiting to come forth in the glorious liberty of God. Long before this takes place, believers will have already experienced the final salvific act at the rapture called the *redemption of our bodies*, which is synonymous with glorification. Then comes the Millennium. After that 1,000-year period has expired, Satan will be loosed from his confinement in the abyss. The devil will then deceive the world's nations to make one final advance on Jerusalem, but God will destroy them with fire from heaven (Rev. 20:7-10). Then the Great White Throne Judgment of the wicked will occur (Rev. 20:11-13). Then the last enemy, which is death, shall be destroyed (1 Cor. 15:26). The new heaven and new earth follow, the final eschatological event before we enter into the eternal age.

And I saw the holy city, new Jerusalem, coming down out of heaven from God, made ready as a bride adorned for her husband.

In New Jerusalem, the city of God, the patriarchs, the saints, the prophets of old, all those of the Church age, along with all the host of heaven, and God Himself, will all live together throughout eternity in the ages to come. We shall see Him as he is (1 John 3:2). We will behold Him face to face (1 Cor. 13:12) as we dwell in New Jerusalem. Here is what the Scriptures say about New Jerusalem.

> The angel who talked with me had a measuring rod of gold to measure the city, its gates and its walls. The city was laid out like a square, as long as it was wide. He measured the city with the rod and found it to be 12,000 stadia in length, and as wide and high as it is long. The angel measured the wall using human measurement, and it was 144 cubits thick. The wall was made of jasper, and the city of pure gold, as pure as glass. The foundations of the city walls were decorated with every kind of precious stone. The first foundation was jasper, the second sapphire, the third agate, the fourth emerald, the fifth onyx, the sixth ruby, the seventh chrysolite, the eighth beryl, the ninth topaz, the tenth turquoise, the eleventh jacinth, and the twelfth amethyst. The twelve gates were twelve pearls, each gate made of a single pearl. The great street of the city was of gold, as pure as transparent glass.
>
> Revelation 21:15-21, NIV

According to this passage, this glorious city will be laid out like a square that is 12,000 stadia (1,400 miles) on all sides. It will be just as high as it is wide. The city will consist of many gems, but most striking is it will be made of transparent gold including the streets. All of this will be greatly enhanced, because "the city had no need of the sun, neither of the moon, to shine in it: for the glory of God did lighten it, and the Lamb *is* the light thereof" (Revelation 21:23, KJV). Imagine how beautiful heaven will be with the light radiating from God Himself as it refracts and reflects off all the gems and through the transparent gold.

God will make everything right. He will wipe away all tears. Death, mourning, and pain will be no more. God will settle all accounts. No one that has ever committed any evil will get away with it. In this life things seem to be so unfair, unjust, unequal, unrighteous, where the rich and affluent seem to get away with their iniquity. Wicked individuals who thought they had evaded justice, God will judge, and they will spend eternity in the lake of fire.

Think about all the pain and despair we experience when a loved one dies, or injustice prevails. At times, hopelessness and depression are unbearable, particularly when evil mocks righteousness and justice. However, the God of all glory shall wipe away the former order where evil is possible. Nothing wicked or evil will enter the gates of New Jerusalem for all eternity. "But the fearful, and unbelieving, and the abominable, and murderers, and whoremongers, and sorcerers, and idolaters, and all liars, shall have their part in the lake which burneth with fire and brimstone: which is the second death" Revelation 21:8, KJV.

All the wicked will pay for their sins. All the righteous will be rewarded. The old order of a fallen world will pass away forever. No matter how dark it gets, or the difficulties you have to go through in life, in the end, God makes it all right. Here is what all believers have to look forward to:

Then he showed me a river of the water of life, clear as crystal, coming from the throne of God and of the Lamb, in the middle of its street. On either side of the river was the tree of life, bearing twelve *kinds of* fruit, yielding its fruit every month; and the leaves of the tree were for the healing of the nations. There will no longer be any curse; and the throne of God and of the Lamb will be in it, and His bond-servants will serve Him; they will see His face, and His name *will be* on their foreheads. And there will no longer be *any* night; and they will not have need of the light of a lamp nor the light of the sun, because the Lord God will illumine them; and they will reign forever and ever. And he said to me, "These words are faithful and true"; and the Lord, the God of the spirits of the prophets, sent His angel to show to His bond-servants the things which must soon take place. "And behold, I am coming quickly. Blessed is he who heeds the words of the prophecy of this book." Revelation 22:1-7

24

What is The Thief in the Night?

The portrayal of the Lord's personal return and the time of judgment called the Day of the Lord are both circumstances to which the phrase *a thief in the night* is applied. Variations of this concept are found in the following passages: Mt. 24:43, 1 Thes. 5:2,4; 2 Peter 3:10, Rev. 3:3, and 16:15 which follows. "Look, I come like a thief! Blessed is the one who stays awake and remains clothed, so as not to go naked and be shamefully exposed" (Rev. 16:15, NIV). To properly understand this metaphorical depiction of the Lord's return requires some unpacking.

As everyone knows, a thief does not announce his coming. As a matter of fact, he purposely comes at a time when no one is expecting. Usually, the opportune time presents itself during the night. The night works well because visibility is restricted, and darkness provides the best cover for hiding. Another advantage presented in the night is that's usually when people are asleep. A sleeping person is unaware of what is going on around him and is cognizant of nothing and presents no resistance.

In the 1 Thessalonians 5 text, the apostle Paul speaking of the Day of the Lord expends further on these metaphors when he writes:

> Now as to the times and the epochs, brethren, you have no need of anything to be written to you. For you yourselves know full well that the day of the Lord will come just like a thief in the night. While they are saying, "Peace and safety!" then destruction will come upon them suddenly like labor pains upon a woman with child, and they will not escape. But you, brethren, are not in darkness, that the day would overtake you like a thief; for you are all sons of light and sons

of day. We are not of night nor of darkness; so then let us not sleep as others do, but let us be alert and sober. For those who sleep do their sleeping at night, and those who get drunk get drunk at night. 1 Thessalonians 5:1-7

Though many use the thief in the night concept to teach that the Lord could come at any time without any warning or signs, this is not what this passage is conveying. It is not so much about the secretness of when He comes but has to do with the people's awareness about the times and seasons that lead up to his coming. Though many have erroneously set out to calculate and predict the day and hour of the Lord's return in the rapture, the Bible emphatically teaches no one knows (Mark 13:32). However, the passage before us is about two different types of people, the children of the day, and those who are in darkness.

Light and dark are metaphors for the saved and the unregenerate. Jesus declared,

This is the judgment, that the Light has come into the world, and men loved the darkness rather than the Light, for their deeds were evil. For everyone who does evil hates the Light, and does not come to the Light for fear that his deeds will be exposed. But he who practices the truth comes to the Light, so that his deeds may be manifested as having been wrought in God." John 3:19-21

In Acts, Paul also emphasizes the dichotomy of the two when making his appeal before King Agrippa when he declares, "…To open their eyes, and to turn them from darkness to light, and from the power of Satan unto God…" (Acts 26:18, KJV). In like manner Peter writes, "But you are a chosen generation, a royal priesthood, a holy nation, His own special people, that you may proclaim the praises of Him who called you out of darkness into His marvelous light" (1 Peter 2:9, NKJV). From these and other passages, we can conclude that darkness is a spiritual condition, whereas sleep is a state of mind, a lack of awareness of things pertaining to the kingdom of God.

On the other hand, the people of God are seen as children of the day, or walking in the light. John also declares, "But if we walk in the light as He is in the light, we have fellowship with one another" (1 John 1:7, NKJV). It is through the fellowship that we have with Him that places us in the light. In other words, those who are born again can see and understand things pertaining to the kingdom of God that require spiritual discernment—things that the natural eye cannot see nor the carnal mind comprehend.

The 1 Thessalonians 5 text says, "For you yourselves know full well that the day of the Lord will come just like a thief in the night. While they are saying, "Peace and safety!" then destruction will come upon them suddenly like labor pains upon a woman with child, and they will not escape." Here, the Day of the Lord is in view, which Paul clearly warns "While they are saying, "Peace and safety!" then destruction will come upon them suddenly." In other words, the children of darkness, who are in a state of "sleep," are not aware of all the signs that the Day of the Lord draws near. They are not aware of all the biblical predictions of the end of the age and all the eschatological prophecies throughout the Old and New Testaments. None of God's Word nor its revelations can be comprehended by those that do not have the spirit of Christ. Therefore, they mock the idea of the Lord's return.

However, the children of the day, true Christians, have the benefit of knowing bible prophecy and being led by the Spirit. Since they are in the light, that day cannot come upon them unaware. Therefore, the apostle writes, "But you, brethren, are not in darkness, that the day would overtake you like a thief; for you are all sons of light and sons of day. We are not of night nor of darkness; so then let us not sleep as others do, but let us be alert and sober." The important takeaway here is the difference between the sleepers and those who are awake, "but let us be alert and sober." If you are watching, the thief cannot sneak up on you. This is why the Lord warned us to "watch."

Take heed, keep on the alert; for you do not know when the appointed time will come. "It is like a man away on a journey, who upon leaving his house and putting his slaves in charge, assigning to each one his task, also commanded the doorkeeper to stay on the alert. "Therefore, be on the alert—for you do not know when the master of the house is coming, whether in the evening, at mid-night, or when the rooster crows, or in the morning—in case he should come suddenly and find you asleep. "What I say to you I say to all, 'Be on the alert!'" Mark 13:33-37

The question is, for what are we to be watching? The answer is simple, for every Bible prophecy given by the Lord about the last days and found in the Scripture. If it's in the Bible, that means that God gave it. If God gave it, that means we are to heed and take it to heart. Here is what the Bible says about prophecy, "Knowing this first, that no prophecy of the scripture is of any private interpretation. For the prophecy came not in old time by the will of man: but holy men of God spake as they were moved by the Holy Ghost" (2 Peter 1:20-21, KJV). Bible prophecies are not the mere whimsical ideations of people. They do not emanate from the depths of men's philosophical pondering or psychoanalytical scrutiny, but as the Spirit of God has revealed, which means they are absolutely infallible.

If God said to watch and be alert, then that is what we must all do. We are all responsible to act on what God has told us. Watch and well as pray. It's true, no one knows the day or the hour of the Lord's return. What this means is that it is not predictable as to the exact day. However, the Bible is clear, you *can* know the season. You can know that it is getting near. You can see what God said to look for. You can know the thief comes at night.

The Bible has a lot to say about the times that are coming on this world. The question is, whose report will you believe? Will you pay attention to what the Lord said to look for? It's not about how many commentaries you read, or what scholar said what. None of that makes a difference, because at the end of the day, all people have to offer is opinions. There-fore, let's close with the Lord's words, "Behold, I am coming like a thief! Blessed is the one who stays awake, keeping his garments on, that he may not go about naked and be seen exposed" (Revelation 16:15, ESV). This is what *the thief in the night* means.

25

WILL THE CHURCH GO "THROUGH"
THE TRIBULATION?

One of the most frequently asked questions concerning end time prophecy is, will the Church go through the tribulation? The answer to this question is complex, because there are many doctrinal views put forth by various scholars and doctrinal camps. Which one of these views you espouse determines how you would answer the question. It is for this very reason that this question is so controversial. However, in order to address this issue, the question requires unpacking, beginning with the word *through*.

According to *Merriam-Webster's Dictionary*, the preposition *through* is "used as a function word to indicate movement into at one side or point and out at another and especially the opposite side of...." With that understanding, the question would be more accurately stated by asking "will the Church go through the entire tribulation." This is what the *going through* question implies. For example, if asked, did you go through the winter? The point of that question is to determine whether you passed through the winter season to the spring.

As discussed in previous chapters, the tribulation is a seven-year period known as Daniel's Seventieth Week. According to Daniel 9:27, in the middle of the Seventieth Week, the Antichrist shall break the covenant that he backed three-and-one-half years earlier. That action kicks off the second half of Daniel's Seventieth Week. This *second half* is the period Jesus identified as "the great tribulation" (Mt. 24:21). So, when the question is asked, will Christians *go through* the tribulation, there is only one rapture position that asserts that point of view, which would be the *post tribulation* rapture position. The others, midtrib and prewrath, teach the rapture happens *before the end* of the tribulation. In that regard, neither of these two positions teaches that the Church goes *through* the tribulation. On the other hand, pretrib teaches that the Church is raptured *before* the Seventieth Week of Daniel or the tribulation begins. This position asserts that the Church does not enter into any part of the tribulation.

Though pretrib is the most popular rapture theory, it may turn out to be the most problematic. One of the reasons it could be problematic is because *what happens if it's wrong.* You see, if the timing of the rapture in the midtrib, posttrib and prewrath views are all wrong, but pretrib is correct, that means the Church is raptured before all the events that follow after the fourth chapter of Revelation. Who's going to complain about that? If we are all gone before the trouble starts, as pretrib teaches, that would certainly be a hallelujah moment for everyone, right? But what if the opposite comes true, and Christians *are not* raptured as pretrib promised before the Seventieth Week arrives? That means believers will be caught flatfooted, and find themselves in the midst of a time they had been promised they would escape, especially when persecution unto death begins.

Many accept pretrib as the right eschatological position. However, they do so without considering, "What would it mean if what pretrib teaches doesn't pan out?" As you continue in this chapter, you will understand why asking "what if pretrib is wrong" is a necessary question. The further out we are from these times, these issues are just subjects to debate. However, the closer we get to these times, it becomes a matter of life and death.

The vast majority of the people do not realize that pretrib is an *eschatological theory* just like all the rest of the positions. Since much of what is written in the Book of Revelation has not happened yet, there is a lot we do not know. Therefore, no matter how widely accepted this rapture position is, that alone does not make it right. Majority acceptance has no determinative power over the outcomes. None of these positions and theories are 100 percent sure, and it mostly boils down to preference as to which position one accepts. However, neither acceptance nor preference is determinative.

Therefore, it is important to approach Revelation without the predispositions that rapture doctrines impose on the text. The first priority should be to hear what the book says, not what dogma says. Ultimately, we must yield to the Bible, not the tenets of our doctrine. Sometimes doctrine can skew the meaning and application of the Scriptures. Jesus addressed the effects of doctrine over Scripture when he rebuked the Pharisees.

> They worship me in vain; their teachings are merely human rules.' You have let go of the commands of God and are holding on to human traditions"... Thus you nullify the word of God by your tradition that you have handed down. And you do many things like that. Mark 7:7-8,13, NIV

In Jesus' rebuke to the scholars of his day, he warns against how doctrines can actually short-circuit the Word of God in people's lives. Not that it invalidates God's Word, because the veracity of Scripture cannot be undone. But the effectiveness in one's life can be altered, diminished, or negated by people's erroneous teaching or misguided interpretations. At this very point is where I urge you to study the Book of Revelation without looking through the tinted lens of *any* particular doctrinal persuasion. In the hearts of many, pretrib is not just a doctrine, but a traditional belief. Beliefs that become traditions are not merely an acknowledgement of something held to be true, but are also passionately defended at a much deeper level. And even if you could demonstrate that a teaching is wrong using Scripture, they would still hold on to their traditional beliefs.

In an attempt to have all the answers, the scholars have enormous power, because they are the ones who shape biblical interpretation for the rest of us, through the seminaries, reference works, commentaries, scholarly articles, and sermonic material, etc. Therefore, just as in Jesus' time, people today typically prefer what the scholars teach even when it contradicts the Scriptures.

A good example of this occurred during a question and answer period when a person asked a top evangelical scholar, Dr. John MacArthur, the following question, "Once a person takes the mark, is there any possibility of him coming to Christ?" Dr. MacArthur's answer was, "I think the answer to that is yes...." The problem here is twofold. Not only does

Dr. MacArthur contradict the clear teaching of the Scriptures, but the second problem is in the question itself. Why ask anyone their opinion on something the Scriptures explicitly declare in the first place? No one's opinion makes a difference when the Scriptures are unambiguous. The passage in question is stated below.

> Then a third angel followed them, saying with a loud voice, "If anyone worships the beast and his image, and receives *his* mark on his forehead or on his hand, he himself shall also drink of the wine of the wrath of God, which is poured out full strength into the cup of His indignation. He shall be tormented with fire and brimstone in the presence of the holy angels and in the presence of the Lamb. And the smoke of their torment ascends forever and ever; and they have no rest day or night, who worship the beast and his image, and whoever receives the mark of his name." Revelation 14:9-11, NKJV

This passage is crystal clear, so why ask the question? Since MacArthur is a well-known scholar who has sold millions of books and commentaries, his words carry weight, because people respect his opinion. But why would anyone place John MacArthur's comments above Scripture, especially when his words contradict what the Scriptures plainly teach? When the Book of Revelation was written, none of these positions and doctrines existed. God didn't need our help. His word is true no matter what our doctrines, traditions, or scholarly opinions assert. "Let God be true but every man a liar" (Rom. 3:4).

God did not give Revelation to validate or establish pretribulationism, or any other system developed by humans. No theologian counseled God on what to say or advised Him on what content to place in Revelation. God gave these sacred words because He chose to reveal His plan for the ages. God's plan is not subject to human eschatology. The veracity of God's word is not subject to rules of Biblical interpretation, nor restricted by dispensational boundaries. This is why sticking to the plain sense of what the Book of Revelation is teaching is so important.

What any pastor or teacher should do is give people what the Word teaches, without being influenced by our doctrinal persuasions. Sow the seed of God's word in people's heart, and let God be responsible for how that seed grows. What we as preachers and teachers try to do with eschatology is sow the seed and assert doctrinal interpretation to control how it grows. But here is what the Bible declares about that.

> What, after all, is Apollos? And what is Paul? Only servants, through whom you came to believe—as the Lord has assigned to each his task. I planted the seed, Apollos watered it, but God has been making it grow. So neither the one who plants nor the one who waters is anything, but only God, who makes things grow.
>
> 1 Corinthians 3:5-7, NIV

Our job as teachers is to teach what Revelation declares without making the same mistake that John MacArthur made when he contradicted what the Scriptures declared, prefaced by these words "*I think....*"

REVELATION'S MESSAGES TO PERSECUTED CHRISTIANS

In the Book of Revelation, there are some clear messages to Christians. For example, the message the Lord gives to the church of Smyrna is thought provoking. "Do not fear what you are about to suffer. Behold, the devil is about to cast some of you into prison, so that you will be tested, and you will have tribulation for ten days. Be faithful until death, and I will give you the crown of life" (Rev. 2:10).

Here, the benefit to this church was *forewarning*, not a promise of deliverance. Forewarning is thematic throughout the entire book and is the main purpose for telling us what will happen ahead of time. Jesus said, "the devil is about to cast some of you into prison." Jesus did not promise "I will stop the devil from throwing you into prison." Incarceration in one of these ancient prisons in itself was often a death sentence. Jesus didn't promise, "Oh, I would never let you go through that." "Before you die, I will come save you." However, what Jesus *did* promise was "Be faithful until death, and I will give you the crown of life."

The fact is that Jesus allowed Satan to cast some of these people into prison, where some of them would suffer and die. How does that message mesh with our doctrines today? Our comfort in this world is not what's at the top of God's list for his saints in this present wicked age. How comfortable we feel about something is not God's standard of measurement.

This is why Jesus highly regards those who give their lives for following Him. Remember, Jesus died too, and he is not asking Christians to do any more that what He did in regards to suffering physical death. Therefore, we cannot let the fear of death control us. Many Christians have died without wavering in their faith.

Jesus warned,

> And I say to you, My friends, do not be afraid of those who kill the body, and after that have no more that they can do. But I will show you whom you should fear: Fear Him who, after He has killed, has power to cast into hell; yes, I say to you, fear Him!
>
> Luke 12:4-5, NKJV

The writer of Hebrews gives us a word of encouragement to move us beyond the bondage of the fear of death.

> Therefore, since the children share in flesh and blood, He Himself likewise also partook of the same, that through death He might render powerless him who had the power of death, that is, the devil, and might free those who through fear of death were subject to slavery all their lives. Hebrews 2:14-15

The fear of death is paralyzing and can enslave a person to such a degree that people will not trust God or his word. Telling people that they will not have to go through tribulation appeases the natural inclination to avoid death because of the fear factor. However, Jesus defeated death and destroyed its ultimate control over those who trust in God. *Foxxe's Book of Martyrs* is full of accounts of Christians that moved beyond the fear of death to embrace the sufferings of Christ. From the very beginning, Christians have picked up their crosses and followed Christ.

Therefore, if there were a thousand Antichrists, the most he could do is kill the body. This is what Revelation says about the Devil's persecution of God's people.

> And I heard a loud voice saying in heaven, Now is come salvation, and strength, and the kingdom of our God, and the power of his Christ: for the accuser of our brethren is cast down, which accused

them before our God day and night. And they overcame him by the blood of the Lamb, and by the word of their testimony; and they loved not their lives unto the death. Rev. 12:10-11, KJV

This passage concerning the saints is one of the most powerful in the Book of Revelation. They overcame Satan through their testimony and through the shed blood of the Lamb. What should be noted is the last part of the verse, "they loved not their lives unto the death." These are Christians that stood for Christ even though it cost them their lives. Self-preservation and the cares of this world were not their priority, because these things will cause you to compromise. They were not in love with their own lives, neither did they love the world more than they loved Christ.

In the face of death, these saints were steadfast and unmovable. Is this a message that is resonating with today's Christians, especially in America? Isn't most of what we are taught today centered around a better self now? Churches in America do not prepare Christians for the level of persecution spoken of by Jesus and John in Revelation. In John's day, believers were all too familiar with martyrdom. How does what the average Christian in America learns in church prepare them for real persecution?

In Matthew, Jesus makes a powerful declaration when He warns,

If anyone desires to come after Me, let him deny himself, and take up his cross, and follow Me. For whoever desires to save his life will lose it, but whoever loses his life for My sake will find it. For what profit is it to a man if he gains the whole world, and loses his own soul? Or what will a man give in exchange for his soul? For the Son of Man will come in the glory of His Father with His angels, and then He will reward each according to his works. Matthew 16:24-27, NKJV

This is a hard message, because it forces you into one of two choices. Either you seek to save your life, thereby losing it, or you lose your life, thereby saving it. This passage also emphasizes a consciousness and a lifestyle of self-sacrifice, denying self and even picking up your own cross, which means because of your faith, you might pay with your life. Today, much of Christian thought is centered around material blessings. But what good does it do if you gain the whole world but lose your soul?

First of all, that reality check that Jesus gave to His disciples is a message for all believers and followers of Christ—pick up your cross! Secondly, this text is eschatological. There is a clear reference to the *Lord's return with His angels to dispense reward according to each person's work.* As we edge closer to Christ's return, how does this message connect to what the average believer is taught about living the prosperous Christian life now?

THE DEFECTION FROM THE FAITH IS COMING

So, why is all of this important, and what does this have to do with the question, *will the Church go through the tribulation?* The answer is, before the Lord returns for the Church, there will be a period of persecution that will cause many to abandon their faith. Hear what the Lord says about this time of tribulation.

> Then you will be handed over to be persecuted and put to death, and you will be hated by all nations because of me. At that time many will turn away from the faith and will betray and hate each other.
> Mt. 24:9-10, NIV

Jesus speaks specifically of a time coming where persecution will become so severe because of His name's sake that it will cause many to defect from the faith. Unlike those in Rev. 12:10-12, these will not be willing to lay down their lives. These will seek to save their lives and, like Jesus warned in Mt. 16:24-27, will end up losing their lives in condemnation.

Paul gives the same warning in 2 Thes. 2:3. "Let no one deceive you by any means; for *that Day will not come* unless the falling away comes first, and the man of sin is revealed, the son of perdition" (NKJV). In this passage, Paul gives a specific instruction speaking of "that day" being the Day of the Lord, not coming until the *falling away,* or the apostasy, occurs. The apostasy is when there will be a mass defection from the faith, in which Jesus and Paul comment.

The *son of perdition* and the *man of sin* are synonyms for the Antichrist. He is the one who is behind the persecution which causes many to fall away. In Revelation, John gives us a different perspective.

> A mouth was given to him to speak boasts and blasphemies.

He was also given authority to act for 42 months. He began to speak blasphemies against God: to blaspheme His name and His dwelling—those who dwell in heaven. And he was permitted to wage war against the saints and to conquer them. He was also given authority over every tribe, people, language, and nation.

Revelation 13:5-7, HCSB

Here the passage informs us that the "beast" (Antichrist) will make war against the *saints*. The word *saint* is from the Greek word *hagios*, which means *sacred, physically pure, morally blameless or religious, ceremoniously consecrated, holy (one or thing) saint* (Strong's Greek Dictionary). It is used sixty-two times in the New Testament, where the vast majority of its applications are to Christians, the saved who are members of the body of Christ. Thirteen of its uses are in the Book of Revelation. It is clear that every use of this word in Acts and the epistles applies to saints who are part of the body of Christ. Therefore, we cannot then change who this word applies to in the Book of Revelation. Saints mean Christians of the body of Christ.

Though the beast kills countless saints in a campaign characterized as a war, hear the words of encouragement to strengthen the saints from wavering under pressure of imprisonment and capital punishment.

If anyone has an ear, he should listen: If anyone is destined for captivity, into captivity he goes. If anyone is to be killed with a sword, with a sword he will be killed. This demands the perseverance and faith of the saints. Revelation 13:9-10, HCSB

Just as Jesus predicted in Mt. 24:9-10, we find the same truth echoed here. So in the plain reading of Scripture, we see that the Antichrist will hate Christians (Jewish or Gentile) and attempt to kill as many as he can get his hands on. He will require the world to take his mark, and the world will do so, all except those whose names are written in the *Lamb's Book of Life*. However, Jesus informs the saints that they will need patience to endure during this time. "All who dwell on the earth will worship him, *everyone* whose name has not been written from the foundation of the world in the book of life of the Lamb who has been slain" (Revelation 13:8). This statement is what distinguishes Christians from those in the world. The saints have their names written in the *Lamb's Book of Life*. This is what Jesus told his disciples when they were rejoicing because they exercised authority over demons. "However, don't rejoice that the spirits submit to you, but rejoice that your names are written in heaven" (Luke 10:20, HCSB).

Once again, the common-sense reading of this text is clear. Those who *refuse* to take the mark of the beast are those Christians whose names are recorded in the *Lamb's book of life written from the foundation of the world.* It is also important to understand that the Antichrist is "permitted" to kill the saints. He cannot do this in and of himself. "And he was *permitted to wage war against the saints* and to conquer them..." (Rev. 13:7, HCSB). God is the one who permits this, because the saints belong to Him. These are those Christians who have united with Christ in his suffering and death. They are being persecuted specifically because they remain faithful to Jesus and have identified with Christ's suffering. Paul states it this way,

> That I may know Him and the power of His resurrection and the fellowship of His sufferings, being conformed to His death; in order that I may attain to the resurrection from the dead.
>
> Philippians 3:10-11

Paul had a self-sacrificing relationship with Christ and accepted being conformed to His suffering and death. This will be the same for those who die under the reign of the Antichrist. Just as Paul was a living sacrifice, so will those who die under the Antichrist be living sacrifices permitted by God to give a great love offering unto the Lord. In Rev. 2:13, Jesus commends a faithful martyr named Antipas. "I know where you live—where Satan has his throne. Yet you remain true to my name. You did not renounce your faith in me, not even in the days of Antipas, my faithful witness, who was put to death in your city—where Satan lives" (Revelation 2:13, NIV). Jesus commends those who remain faithful, particularly under extreme circumstances such as faced during the tribulation. This is why it is stated of these same glorious saints, whom pretrib declares to be *left behinds*, a ridiculous characterization popularized by the *Left Behind* book series and movie. These noble saints "...loved not their lives even unto the death..." (Rev. 12:11).

Let us also consider Stephen when he was being stoned, a brutal and barbaric way to die.

When the members of the Sanhedrin heard this, they were furious and gnashed their teeth at him. But Stephen, full of the Holy Spirit, looked up to heaven and saw the glory of God, and Jesus standing at the right hand of God. "Look," he said, "I see heaven open and the Son of Man standing at the right hand of God." At this they covered their ears and, yelling at the top of their voices, they all rushed at him, dragged him out of the city and began to stone him. Meanwhile, the witnesses laid their coats at the feet of a young man named Saul. While they were stoning him, Stephen prayed, "Lord Jesus, receive my spirit." Then he fell on his knees and cried out, "Lord, do not hold this sin against them." When he had said this, he fell asleep.

Acts 7:54-59, NIV

How is it that Christians in New Testament times had this type of faith but Christians today in America do not? How many Christians do you know that want to be conformed to Christ's death and have fellowship with his sufferings? How many times have you heard the following passage, preached or taught in church?

Without being frightened in any way by those who oppose you. This is a sign to them that they will be destroyed, but that you will be saved—and that by God. For it has been granted to you on behalf of Christ not only to believe in him, but also to suffer for him...

Philippians 1:28-29, NIV

This passage declares, "For it has been granted to you...." In other words, by divine grace, God has allowed you to be partakers in Christ's suffering, which in the sight of God is glorious. "Precious in the sight of the LORD *Is* the death of His saints" (Psalm 116:15, NKJV). Does this mean we should walk around with a death wish? Of course not! However, we should live with this understanding that your faith can cause you to make the ultimate sacrifice. Although we haven't yet seen this type of persecution in America, many Christians around the world serve Christ under the threat of death.

According to a study conducted by *The Center for Study of Global Christianity,* between the years 2005 and 2015, over 900,000 Christians, averaging 90,000 per year, were martyred around the world. Only in the West do Christians have the luxury of saying, "Oh we'll be raptured before all of that starts happening. God would not let us go through what other Christians are experiencing." However, history does not come close to bearing that out. Christians have always died for the faith, and will continue to do so. Most Americans have been spoiled by a Christianity of convenience.

In Rev. 14, we find another powerful message to Christians during the time of the Antichrist's tyrannical reign.

> And the smoke of their torment will rise for ever and ever. There will be no rest day or night for those who worship the beast and its image, or for anyone who receives the mark of its name." This calls for patient endurance on the part of the people of God who keep his commands and remain faithful to Jesus. Then I heard a voice from heaven say, "Write this: Blessed are the dead who die in the Lord from now on." "Yes," says the Spirit, "they will rest from their labor, for their deeds will follow them." Revelation 14:11-13, NIV

This passage is very interesting. A special exhortation heralded by an angel to believers to encourage them not to give in to the intense pressure to take the mark of the beast. The pressure will be enormous to give in and conform. It must be emphasized that the world will love the Antichrist. Those who fail to comply will be seen by the world as traitors and nonconformists, who are to be jailed and sentenced to die. But it will be eternally worthwhile to obey God. Therefore, the exhortation is given, "This calls for patient endurance on the part of the people of God who keep his commands and remain faithful to Jesus."

The plain reading of that passage is obvious. These are Christians. These are not some group of left behinds who didn't make the cut to be in the rapture. The only way to walk away with that interpretation, is that you must impose dispensational, pretrib doctrinal tenets onto this text. At this point, pretrib is forced to assign this group of saints to a second-class status as those who were not righteous enough to be raptured. Now, being left behind, they must prove their loyalty by being martyred. Here pretribulationist short-circuits the plain meaning of the text, and must create the left behind narrative as the only way to explain that there are still Christians whose names are written in the Lamb's Book of Life on earth during the time of the Antichrist.

Instead of today's Christians understanding what is going to happen to the Church, they have been taught that none of this applies to the Church. God has given the forewarning concerning things to come, but many won't heed or be prepared for what is going to happen, because their hope is in a problematic theological position that teaches that the Church won't be on earth during this time. What a sad commentary.

The next aspect of this passage is even more compelling. "Then I heard a voice from heaven say, "Write this: Blessed are the dead who die in the Lord from now on." "Yes," says the Spirit, "they will rest from their labor, for their deeds will follow them."

Here again, we have another statement made from heaven that if you understand it from its plain reading (perspicuity of the Scriptures) reveals more important truths. From heaven it is declared, "Blessed are the dead who die in the Lord from now on," is one of seven beatitudes of Revelation (Rev. 1:3, 16:15, 19:9, 20:6, 22:7, 22:14). Here the blessedness is directed towards those who die "in the Lord" or "in Christ" who will be martyred during the time of the Antichrist. Notice these Christians' status, they "die *in* the Lord." Being "in Christ" is a positional reality that is found in the Pauline epistles. Believers are united with Christ through baptism by the Holy Spirit into the body of Christ (1 Cor. 12:13). It is important to note that they die *in the Lord*, emphasizing the fact that the baptizing ministry of the Holy Spirit is still active.

On the other hand, the pretribulationist is committed to the doctrinal proposition that the Holy Spirit has been taken from the earth as the restrainer, and is no longer baptizing believers into the body of Christ. This forces an illegitimate identification on most of the "saint" narratives in Revelation as being not the Church, but tribulation saints, thus short-circuiting the intent of the Scriptures to inform the Church of that time.

The final aspect of this passage is a surprise exclamation by the Holy Spirit Himself, when he responds to the blessedness of those who die in the Lord, "Yes," says the Spirit, "they will rest from their labor, for their deeds will follow them." The plain reading of this text, once again, confirms that the Holy Spirit is quite active during this time. In His role as the Comforter, He gives comfort to those who die in Christ by confirming by way of exclamation that their sacrifice will not be forgotten in heaven, because their works will follow them. Though pretrib declares these saints to be the left behinds, a second-class status, those who didn't make the rapture cut, God sees them as first-class and so noteworthy that this is one of a few times the Holy Spirit speaks in Revelation.

Many pretribulationist claim that the rapture doctrine is to inspire comfort based on an interpretation of 1 Thes. 4:18. Sarcastically they ask, "What comfort would it be, if the Church was still here to be martyred by the Antichrist? Where is the comfort in that?" This is one of the reasons they used to reject the idea that the Church is still here during the reign of the Antichrist. However, Rev. 14:13 blows that assertion out of the water, because the Comforter Himself is the one guaranteeing the saints who are martyred that they will be remembered in eternity for their labor. How much more comforting can you get when the Holy Spirit Himself affirms the blessedness of those who die in the Lord? That's true comfort! Though there are those who claim the saints of Revelation are *other than* the Church, as we have seen, the plain reading of the Scriptures does not back up that assertion.

It has been the purpose of this last chapter to drive home one defining point: When Revelation is read without any help from an eschatological doctrine, the message God intended gets through. Revelation was written during the close of the first century in 90 A.D. However, the dispensationalism of today would not influence the interpretation of Revelation until the nineteenth century. Once dispensationalism came to America, introduced by John Nelson Darby in the 1830s, it would later be propagated around the world through the *Scofield Reference Bible* in 1909, and then in later editions. The Scofield is still widely used to this day.

So, is the Church still on earth during the reign of the Antichrist? Yes, it is! Though pretrib designates these believers as another group of saints, it is important to understand that Revelation makes no such distinction. Dispensational scholars declare them to be different, not the Bible. Some also claim that since the word church is not found in Revelation after chapter 3 and is not mentioned again until chapter 22 is another proof that the Church has been raptured. However, that is a superficial argument. In Galatians, the word church(es) is used in the first chapter but not used again. In 1 Thessalonians the word church(es) is used in the first and second chapters but not used again. Should it be concluded that the rest of Galatians and Thessalonians does not apply to Christians or to the body of Christ because the word church is not used after a certain point? Of course not!

In Revelation, the Lord was addressing seven specific churches in Asia Minor, which is modern-day Turkey (see Rev. 1:4, 1:11). Each church had specific characteristics and issues, and received different rebukes, admonitions, and commendations. Specific individuals such as Antipas were named, and particular doctrinal issues cited. In that sense Revelation is partly historical. However, once we come to the futuristic aspects of Revelation, such as the mark of the beast, by that time, and as it is now, the Church is a worldwide organism that is no longer regional. With literally millions of churches worldwide and thousands of denominations, the Church can no longer be called out individually or by location.

However, there are more problems with that argument. The word *church* is also not found in 2 Timothy, Titus, 2 Peter, 1 & 2 John, and Jude. 1 Peter should be included as well, because in the KJV, in the phrase "church at Babylon" (1 Pet. 5:13), *church* is italicized, meaning that it was added by the translators and not in the original text. Pretribulationist never point this out whenever they make that argument. Should we conclude that the Church not being mentioned means that the epistles cited, their material does not apply to Christians? Or, that because the word *church* is not found in this list of epistles that should be interpreted as what is written in these epistles does not apply to the Church? If that were to be the interpretive rule, then we would also have to say seven New Testament books do not apply to the Church either. Of course, that would be ridiculous, just as is that pretrib argument. Paul did not only refer to Christians as the Church, he also used the word *saints*, as does John.

Additionally, John only uses the word *church* in a local sense. Neither John nor any other writer in the epistles, with the exception of Hebrews, uses the word *church* in other than a local sense. Paul was the one who received the revelation of the Church being the body of Christ. Paul emphatically declared that he did not receive his doctrine from people, but by revelation of Jesus Christ (see Gal. 1:11-12). Therefore, we should not expect to see, nor do we see, terminology exclusively used by Paul in other epistles.

When John is speaking of the marriage supper of the Lamb, he speaks of the Lamb's wife (a metaphor for the church) being made ready and clothed in white linen. John specifically says that the white linen represents *the righteousness of the saints* (see Rev. 19:8). He does not use Pauline terminology and say *righteousness of the church*. On the other hand, Paul, when speaking of the relationship between a husband and a wife, applies that analogy to the relationship that Christ has with the Church. Paul declares, "That he might present himself a glorious church without spot or wrinkle." Paul uses *church*, John uses *saints*, but it's the same body of believers.

Considering all that has been said in this chapter, it is not the author's intention to change anyone's mind. Doctrines and traditions are tenaciously guarded. However, it is vitally important to understand that there is more to Revelation than how pretrib interprets it. When Revelation was written, none of these doctrinal schemes existed. This means the Word of God is not dependent upon these and can stand on its own. Therefore, you should engage Revelation without the doctrinal conditions. Read the book. Let Revelation speak directly to your spirit. It is the only book in the Bible that has a specific blessing for reading and taking to heart the things that are written therein. Know that God did not give this book for only scholars to understand. The book is written to "he that has an ear...."

Through its inspired pages, the Lord encourages his saints that no matter what happens, those who remain faithful to Jesus are victorious in the end, whether it be in life or death. As Paul declared to the church at Philippi, "For me, living is Christ and dying is gain... I have the desire to depart and be with Christ—which is far better" (Phil. 1:21,23, HCSB). When it was time for Paul to be beheaded, this was his attitude.

> For I am already being poured out as a drink offering, and the time for my departure is close. I have fought the good fight, I have finished the race, I have kept the faith. There is reserved for me in the future the crown of righteousness, which the Lord, the righteous Judge, will give me on that day, and not only to me, but to all those who have loved His appearing. 2 Tim. 4:6-8, HCSB.

The drink offering was wine that was poured over a sacrifice before it was to be burned. Paul likened himself to the drink offering, because he knew he was going to be beheaded. He stood steadfast in the face of martyrdom, rebuffing an escapist mentality. He embraced dying as an offering to the Lord that redeemed him. In this way, he experienced the fellowship with Christ's suffering and death in order to know Him in the power of His resurrection. Do Christians in the West and in America have this mentality? No! We haven't been taught this aspect of what it means to be a Christian. However, as we get closer to the time, we must start having this conversation.

The pretribulational rapture theory will be proven wrong once the treaty prophesied in Daniel 9:27 occurs and the Church is still here. Another marker will be once construction on the temple in Jerusalem starts and is completed, and the rapture hasn't occurred, we'll know pretrib is wrong. Pretribulationist insist that the building of the temple will occur during the Seventieth Week. When these events occur, everyone will know pretrib is false.

At that point, the important thing to remember is that God's Word has not failed, but the pretrib theory has. Do not believe anyone that says you can take the mark of the beast and still be saved. At that time, the Church of Jesus Christ will have to hunker down and remain steadfast. During those times, the exhortation found in Revelation 14:12 will help keep us steady. "This calls for patient endurance on the part of the people of God who keep his commands and remain faithful to Jesus" (NIV).

Finally, when the author asks, *what if pretrib is wrong*, this is not a hypothetical question. There is solid biblical proof that undermines what pretrib teaches. For the most comprehensive and compelling arguments exposing the weaknesses of pretribulationism, please refer to the author's book titled *Revelation Revolution, the Antichrist, Angels, and the Abyss.*

About the Author

Dr. Dennis J. Woods has studied eschatology for over 40 years. His fascination with biblical prophecy began in 1976 after reading his first Hal Lindsey book while serving in the Navy on board the U.S.S. England. In 1982, after being honorably discharged, he continued his eschatological studies, reading several dispensational authors and scholars.

In 1994, Dr. Woods' first book Unlocking the Door: A Key to Biblical Prophecy was published, giving him national exposure. In 1995, he further sharpened his eschatological skills by taking a Revelation course taught by renowned New Testament theologian Dr. D.A. Carson, at *Trinity Evangelical Divinity School*, Wisconsin extension, Elm Brook Church. In 1996, he also corresponded with and challenged Dallas Theological Seminary pillars Dr. John Walvoord (2004) and in 1997, J. Dwight Pentecost (2014).

Today, Dr. Woods is President and CEO of Life To Legacy, LLC a thriving independent book publisher having published numerous titles for various authors. He is also the pastor of Power of the Holy Ghost Deliverance Ministries, with a radio outreach ministry in Chicago IL. Dr. Woods also has the Revelation Revolution Podcast. For their spiritual enrichment he and his wife of over 20 years Chantia, attend the Apostolic Church of God, of Chicago Illinois, where Dr. Byron T. Brazier is the pastor.

In 2004, Dr. Woods received his Doctorate of Biblical Studies from Midwest Theological Institute of Indiana.

All speaking engagement requests should be submitted to:

Life2legacybooks@att.net

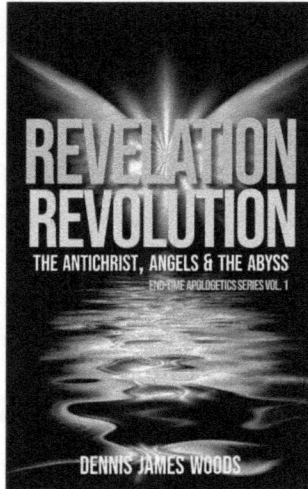

The book of Revelation is the most mysterious and controversial book in the Bible. Yet, God intended that Christians be enriched by its enduring message. However, many believers do not read Revelation. Could one reason be they have been taught that most of Revelation does not apply to the Church? In this first volume of *The End Time Apologetics Series*, the author challenges the Pretribulation rapture position and uncovers how many Christians may not be prepared for prophetic events to come. Though many tout pretrib as a fact, in reality, it is "theory" that gained traction in America in the 19th century. Further popularized after being published in an immensely popular reference bible, pre-trib quickly become the preferred rapture position. As we witness the fulfillment of prophetic events around the world, the real question is "What happens if the pre-trib rapture theory is wrong?" Would modern day Christians remain faithful under persecution as have past generations of Church saints?

In this powerful book, discover how facts concerning the Antichrist, Angels, and the Abyss, are a game-changer for the pretribulation rapture position. Learn what effect it would have if the Holy Spirit is not the restrainer of Second Thessalonians. See actual correspondence between the author and two of the most esteemed Dispensational scholars who made some surprising admissions about who's really restraining the Antichrist. Will end time events actually turn out as portrayed in the Left Behind series? Will Christians be prepared for the perilous times to come? What could trigger the great falling away? Be forewarned, those who have ears, let them hear what the Spirit says to Christians concerning the Antichrist, Angels, and the Abyss.

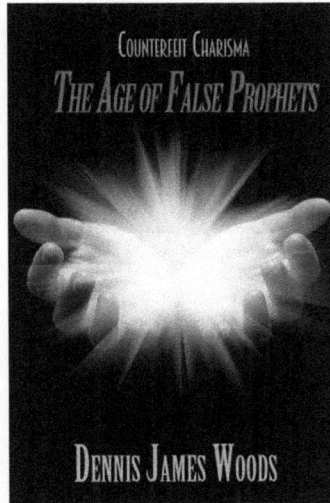

A wave of curiosity in the prophetic ministry is sweeping up many in a deluge of deception. This counterfeit movement may be among the ominous signs of the last days. An obsession with "prophecy, signs, and wonders" can contribute to an unhealthy attraction to anything determined to be supernatural. In Matthew 16:4, Jesus declared, "A wicked and adulterous generation seeks after a sign...." False prophets amaze people by calling out phone numbers, addresses and declaring meaningless prophecies. However, unknown to the masses, false prophets use divination, the same power fortune-tellers and psychics have used for centuries.

This thought-provoking book examines actual cases of false prophets in action revealing their secrets and subterfuge. You will learn what a legitimate prophetic message is and the specific characteristics to detect false prophecies. You will also discover how people that have itching ears for "a prophetic word" and lust after wealth, create an environment for false prophets to thrive. This powerful book also investigates the legitimacy of the "schools of prophets," and how some of these schools teach mystical arts. Even if you attend a church where false prophets are not going forth, they still have a commanding presence on the internet and enter households through popular social media sites. The Bible warns, "My people are destroyed from the lack of knowledge!" Therefore, be informed and forewarned, because false prophecy could be creeping into your home or coming to a church near you!

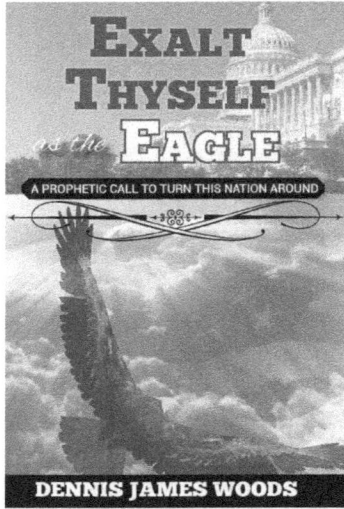

Exalt Thyself as the Eagle, is a thought provoking book that reveals how the prophecies of Obadiah bear a remarkable resemblance to characteristics of the United States. From the words of the most mysterious prophet of the Bible, this eye-opening examination pinpoints prophetic parallels between the ancient Edomites and modern day Americans. Though his prophecy is only twenty-one verses in length, the book of Obadiah packs a powerful end-time message that cannot be ignored. Learn how the power, prestige and pride of Esau's descendants, were foreshadows for the economic, moral and military decline of United States. You will be amazed to discover that America's national symbol, high standard of living, and presence in outer space are not coincidental, but were foreshadowed in Obadiah over twenty-five-hundred years ago. If America is to be saved from the consequences of her actions, there must be national repentance from the White House down. "Exalt Thyself as the Eagle" is the clarion call for America's most precious resource—the Church—to stand up and be counted to ignite the spark of revival—to turn this nation around!

About the Publisher

Let *Life to Legacy* bring your story to literary life! We offer the following publishing services: manuscript development, editing, transcription services, ghost-writing, cover design, copyright services, ISBN assignment, worldwide distribution, and eBook conversion.

We make the publishing process easy. Throughout production, we keep the author informed every step of the way. Even if you do not have a manuscript, that's not a problem for us. We can ghost-write your book from audio recordings or legible handwritten documents. Whether print-on-demand or trade publishing, we have packages to meet your publishing needs. At *Life to Legacy*, we take the stress out of becoming a published author.

Unlike other *so-called* publishers, we do more than just print books. Our books and eBooks are distributed to book buyers, distributors, and online retailers throughout the world. This is real publishing! Call us today for a free quote.

Please visit our website
www.Life2Legacy.com

or call us
877-267-7477

Send email inquiries
Life2Legacybooks@att.net